A SUSSEX WAYFARER'S

NATURE NOTES

David Johnston

OAKBARN
PRESS

© 2016 David Johnston
A Sussex Wayfarer's Nature Notes

ISBN 978-0-9955581-0-6

Published by OakBarn Press
16 Orchard Close
Petworth
West Sussex GU28 0SA

The right of David Johnston to be identified as the author of this work has been asserted by him in accordance with the Copyright, Designs and Patents Act 1988.

A CIP catalogue record of this book
can be obtained from the British Library.

Book designed by Michael Walsh at
The Better Book Company • 5 Lime Close • Chichester PO19 6SW

and printed by
4edge • 7a Eldon Way • Hockley • Essex SS5 4AD

david.rg.johnston@googlemail.com
www.davidjohnston.org.uk

Front cover picture: – St. Christopher (patron Saint of wayfarers) which stands at the foot of Treyford Hill, Nr West Harting.

Other books by the same author:-

'West Sussex Barns and Farm Buildings'
'City Streets to Sussex Lanes'
'The Restless Miller'

During his nature walks, David captured many hundreds of images of the Sussex countryside. These photographs built up to a massive archive of 35mm slides: 6,000 of which have now gone into the hands of the West Sussex Record Office – now available under the title:-

The David Johnston Countryside Collection: Sussex Barns
The David Johnston Collection of West Sussex Landscape Photographs

This book would not have been possible without the great patience of my wife Sue – my constant companion; my dearest friend; my additional eyes and ears, and my ever-ready source of knowledge throughout these Sussex Nature excursions.

My ever grateful thanks to Michael Walsh of The Better Book Company for all his help and expertise in the skilled design and final production of this book.

This compendium of countryside observations is dedicated to Sue.

FOREWORD

My nomadic wanderings have, over the past thirty years, taken me through a myriad of field paths in the county of Sussex; and out there, during that time, I have often been captivated by the awesome beauty of the countryside. Only the other day, as I lingered by an old farm gate on the north side of the Downs, I unexpectedly found my imagination teased by the gentle movement of sheep grazing in the meadow before me – the fascination being, that the whole flock were half consumed in a silver sea of gossamers. The air was still – cold, typical of autumn – the afternoon sun casting elongated shadows across the distant landscape – and there I stood wholly immersed in this bewitching scene, the marvel of which was amplified the more by that primeval silence which occasionally rests upon the South Downs.

How long I was held under the spell of this natural phenomenon, I cannot say – probably no more than a few minutes – but suddenly, the hush was broken by the clamour of rooks squabbling over by the hillside – I altered my gaze in that direction. Then, I swung round and made my way out across the broad open field, breathing in the sweet Downland air as I went.

Soon, I stumbled on a sunken lane; and there I came to a halt, having decided, that it was far too late in the day to go further. So I lingered awhile, to watch the dwindling sun-rays light up the hedgerows – the old-man's-beard, and the gossamers which trailed out and across the path, like delicate strands of glass. It was a glorious moment – the likes of which have, in the past, been a constant inspiration in the writing of my Sussex Nature Notes. But in stark contrast to these peaceful moments, there is too, chronicled in my diaries – floods, blizzards and the devastating effect that the great storm of 1987 had on the countryside. The following photographs show a snippet of the '87 storm destruction.

Above: Inholmes Wood, Stoughton – before the 1987 great storm

Below: Inholmes Wood, after 1987 great storm – photo taken from the same position as above picture.

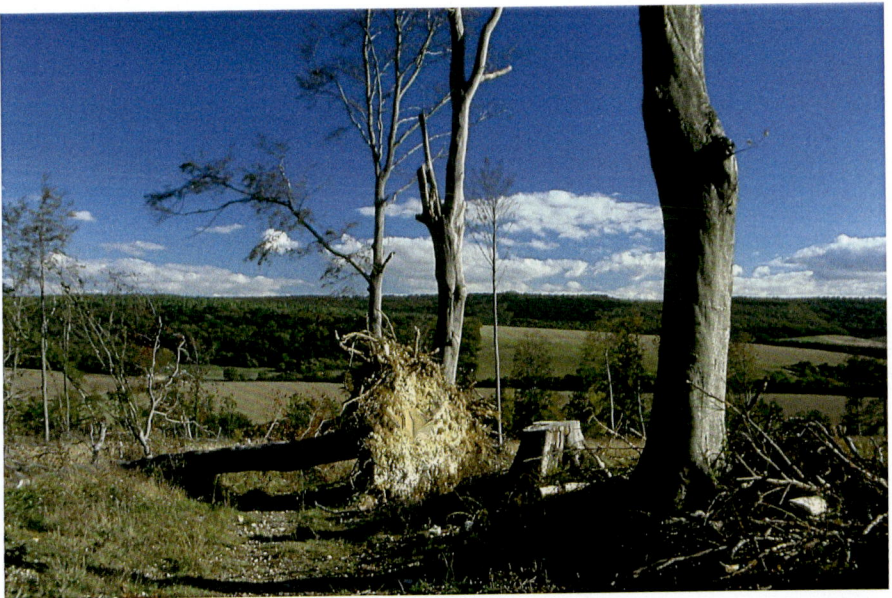

PREFACE

By David Arscott, former BBC Radio Sussex producer and presenter and the author of some 40 books about Sussex.

Diary writing is, one imagines, out of fashion, save among politicians and other public figures who have an eye to profiting from it. The manifold pressures of life, together with the lure of online platforms such as Facebook and Twitter which encourage instant public posturings, have conspired to relegate the creation of a daily record of humdrum life to the realm of arcane, almost furtive pastimes such as model-making and train-spotting. How regrettable this is will be discovered by anyone turning the pages of David Johnston's richly evocative record of rural life in the years before and immediately after the millennium.

Those of us who share his love of 'ordinary' Sussex countryside will find ourselves happily carried away to small, sequestered corners of it, where we rejoice in his vivid description of birds, beasts and flowers. And although the opening of these diaries is but three decades away, we will also find ourselves regretting what has been lost or sadly diminished in that short space of time.

Recent years have seen a flourishing of self-consciously literary accounts of landscapes both urban and rural, but David Johnston's writing is part of an older tradition. Here we come across no grand theorising, no challenging vocabulary, no highfalutin' showing off, but a direct use of language which creates distinct little worlds of sight, sound and smell. To read these daily snippets is to be inspired to put on our walking boots, take up our binoculars and explore the countryside afresh.

A SUSSEX WAYFARER'S NATURE NOTES

Any words interpolated into the text of the Diary itself for explanation are shown in square brackets [ ]; ordinary brackets ( ) are those that were used when the Diary was first written.

1987

2nd January – [Stoughton] We went for a walk over by the Woodman's cottage: wandered through the woods [Lordington Copse] to the far side, then out to a small patch of wasteland; there we found an old shepherd's hut. Hazel catkins are out; teasels abound in this acre of ragged grassland – the undergrowth – thick as a jungle.

3rd January – [Compton, West Sussex.] We took a walk through Haslett Copse: tramped through the woods to the Keepers Cottage, then crossed over the road and into the field – many fossilised shells scattered about here – found a shepherds crown [fossilised mollusc.] Lovely sunny day – stopped here for a picnic. Saw a deer in the woods, and a weasel.

8th January – [Stoughton]Went over to the Woodman's, walked through the woods and out to the wild, overgrown meadow – sun glistened on the pretty stream that winds through the vale – fields covered in mist, a most beautiful sight. Spotted a rabbit nibbling grass beside a tree. It was a lovely sunny day, although cold; frost lay about the countryside all day long. Some of my photographs, along with an article I had written appear in the 'West Sussex Gazette.'

14th January – Heavy snowfall during the night – bitterly cold wind – snowed all day. Did not venture out – spent the day sorting through photos and writing.

15th January – [Stoughton] We took a rather treacherous drive over towards Racton the roads snowbound all the way – hedgerows covered by drifts five to six feet high – all most picturesque: I took several photos. Wind still bitterly cold.

16th January – [Compton, West Sussex] Not so cold today – had no more snow. We went over to Compton. Beautiful snowdrifts between Stoughton and Marden: milk lorry stuck in snow. We climbed to the top of Compton Hill – deep drifts up there – I took photos of the scenery – had great fun sledging on the hill.

26th January – [Stoughton] Went for a walk over Stansted: tramped up the lane towards the old orchard, then on through the woods and back round the fields. Still a lot of snow about. Lovely walk – weather dry and mild.

28th January – [Prinsted Harbour, West Sussex.] We took a walk down Prinsted, strolled along the shore. Hundreds of Canada geese in the outlying fields. Weather was cold but sunny; a chill sea breeze – nice and refreshing.

31st January – [Stoughton.] Went over to Inholmes Wood for a walk – saw about a dozen deer bolting through the woods – I managed to get a photo of them. We came out onto the open meadows; stopped for hot tea from our flask – breathtaking views looking down the valley – the old Racton Tower, the sea misty in the distance. Snow still lies about the fields in patches.

5th February – [Stoughton.] Went for a walk over Stansted: hazel catkins are out – blankets of snowdrops too, all in full bloom in the woods. Weather, dull, misty but mild – days are getting longer, still light at 5 o'clock.

19th February – [Marden.] Went over to North Marden were we walked down the hill to the far end of the field – took a photo of the old shepherds hut that lies down there – it's falling into ruin fast. Spotted a dozen or more deer over by the farm. Weather – sunny, but cold.

22nd February – [Compton, West Sussex.] Went over to Markwells Wood, near Deanlane End; beautiful country lanes; came to a lovely old farm; and a tiny, derelict cottage hidden in the woods – took several photos of it. Saw about twenty deer. We must have tramped half a dozen miles today. Weather chill – snow still lies about in places. Beautiful walk – we came home with rosy cheeks.

7th March – [Stoughton.]Went over to Stansted, near Chichester. It started snowing – very hard. Took some pictures of the snowdrops and wild daffodils in the woods. Snow turned to slush by evening.

A most horrific accident in the English channel – the Townsend Thoresen ferry, the 'Zeebrugge' sank last night – 100 feared dead, 150 in hospital – the boat turned on its side and sank in 10 seconds.

11th March – [Stoughton.] Went over to Forestside for a walk – came to an old ruin in the woods, probably a long since redundant lime kiln. Found close by it, an old rusting, cast iron trivet, with all the signs of the zodiac impressed into it – a most interesting relic. A lovely ramble – beautiful sunny day – I took a number of pictures of pheasants that strutted about the hedgerows.

14th March – We went over to West Marden, for a walk – the pussy willow is out – first we've seen this year. Wandered through the woods to the open fields; and there we tucked into our sandwiches – all so quiet; so very peaceful. Saw a fox, it trotted close by us as we ate our lunch – he was no more than 20 or 30 feet away. A most wonderful day for all kinds of nature – we spotted about sixteen deer; a jay; two rabbits; a magpie; and a green woodpecker. We walked to Southholt Farm, and back – beautiful sunny day, quite mild.

26th April – [Marden.] Went over to Lower Farm, Up Marden, where we walked up the lane, and past the farm cottages towards Wildham Barn. Sat on an old fallen tree stump for perhaps, a couple of hours – beautiful hot sunny day – Isle of Wight stood out clearly in the distance; a sure sign of bad weather to come – so they say. After a while, we sauntered on over to the woods, where we listened to the birds singing their heart out – a lovely peaceful, beautiful day. In the evening, we tramped up to Racton Tower, and watched the sun go down in a red blaze of glory.

28th June – Went over to West Marden, where we walked up the old lane, past Horsley Farm and on through Markwells wood, to South Holt Farm: saw a baby thrush in the hedge by the cowsheds. We wandered on down the lane and past the old keepers cottage: saw a few rabbits – noticed too, half a dozen deer foraging in the copse: dog roses out in profusion. Beautiful walk – must have covered about six miles today.

29th June – [Stoughton.] Went for a walk up by the old woodman's cottage, [Monarch's Way,] wandered through the woods [Lordington Copse] where we found hoards of early purple orchids. Disturbed a deer that had been lying in the long grass in the old meadow. Lovely warm sunny day.

24th July – [Stoughton.] Went to Forestside, and strolled up the lane, towards Warren Down. Saw a foal in the field. Sat and had a picnic: then we walked on down the long meadow – lots of wild flowers and herbs; rosebay-willow-herb looked lovely. Hoards of butterflies: all so very peaceful.

29th July – [Chalton, Hampshire.] Went to Idsworth church, [St. Hubert's,] to see the wall paintings. Beautiful little chapel situated in the middle of a field. Walked up through Heberdens Farm, opposite the church – can see for miles from the top of the hill. Lots of butterflies about – various species of blues and small fritillaries: numerous wild flowers.

31st July – [Compton, West Sussex] Went for a walk over Inholmes Wood. Saw a green woodpecker: took several photos of butterflies, including the comma.

3rd August – [Stoughton.] Walked through Stansted woods, then on up the lane to the old house, just past the orchard: found some chicory. Wandered through the hazel copse and out by Sindles Farm, Aldsworth. The old farmer [John Velton] was leaning over the farmyard gate – in thoughtful mood. We got talking to him – a most interesting gentleman: he told me of his passion for studying the numerous moths on his farm. He had made a light-box out of a used egg-box – which he placed in his meadows. The purpose being, to catch the moths which had been attracted overnight to the light, and hence, settled in it – he then photographed the various species; after which, he released them unharmed, back into the wild.

8th August – [Treyford.] We set off on our walk from The Royal Oak, at Hooksway: found lots of flowers: saw an adder; some large puffballs in a field; also pyramid orchids; harebells and scabious. Walked by Philliswood Farm, then on past Buriton Farm, and back towards The

Royal Oak. It was late afternoon by the time we got back there, and the old pub was closed – all was quiet. Even the noise of traffic, I noticed, could not reach this tiny, hidden hamlet. A lovely ramble today – though the weather was cloudy. [There is an old belief that Hooksway, is so called, after a seventeenth century smuggler who used to use the Royal Oak as a halfway house for his contraband. He would come with his pack-horses from Portsmouth, down to this secluded nook, and then on and up over the Downs to Cocking, and so to Midhurst. Once there, he would go directly to Knock Hundred Row, where he always stored his illicit goods in the secret passages and attics within.]

9th August – [near Marden – Sussex / Hampshire border.] Went over to Idsworth: walked up to the quaint old church in the field – met there, the church warden who told us that the village which had once stood there, had been wiped out by the black death. We wandered on up the hill and had a picnic: beautiful views looking over towards the Isle of Wight. Tramped up over the down, then made our way back to the field again – quite sunny and warm. As we were climbing over the stile, we noticed, on the wooden rail, a newt [a snake eyed skink] a lovely little creature – it sat motionless long enough for me to take a photograph.

10th August – [Sussex / Hampshire border.] We went over to Idsworth, and climbed the hill that lies on the other side of the railway tracks. An abundance of butterflies over there – various species of blues and small fritillaries – these meadows being an ideal habitat: hoards of wild flowers.

14th August – [Sussex / Hampshire border.] Went over to Charlton Down – found a small companula: photographed two or three of the many brimstone butterflies that were about today.

16th August – [Chalton, Sussex / Hampshire border.] Went to Chalton Down and walked up and over the hill to Chalton Church and village, then turned back towards Idsworth, we sat on the downs in the sunshine and had a picnic. Saw an elephant hawk moth caterpillar and a clouded yellow butterfly. We then wandered up the path towards Ditcham Park, where we saw a pair of mole crickets.

19th August – [Harting.] We set off from Harting – climbed the path that leads up through the hanger to the top of the hill, to look at the Vandelian Tower, which I photographed. I also took pictures of stubble burning in the distance. The views from the tower are stunning, can see as far as the Isle of Wight.

20th August – [Harting.] Went for a walk over to Hucksholt Farm, and along path to Ladyholt; then on and round towards Eckensfield; where a house close by, had been gutted out by builders, for the purpose of modernisation. It was built c. 1710? – had some very old beams, and a wonderful inglenook fireplace. From here, we wandered on over to Compton Down; and there had a picnic – 'under the Greenwood Tree' – amongst a whole host of scabious and harebells – a perfect picture in the downland grass. Found, in a ploughed field on the crest of the hill, several well preserved, 'shepherds crowns' [fossilised mollusc]. Spotted 3 deer about 10 feet away. Very warm sunny day.

27th August – [Harting] Went over to Woodcroft Farm, and walked up Harris lane to Ladyholt, (near South Harting.) A tractor driver who was busy working in a field, stopped and chatted a while – he told us where to find the old 'well' where the Hawkhurst gang, drowned the excise man, William Chater. Woodcroft farm, teams with wildlife – saw a tiny shrew, some willow warblers, house martins; a hawk and many species of butterflies: took some photos of giant dragonflies.

5th September – [Idsworth: Sussex / Hampshire border] Went for a walk up past Heberden Farm – sat on the hill for some long time, taking in the wonderful views – the Isle of Wight in the distance. Came over black and stormy after a while – started to thunder; but soon cleared over. Back to car, and drove to Woodcroft Farm – saw the farmer [Mike Millington] with his Shire horse – held in harness – I took several photos of him.

14th September – Went over to Harting, walked up towards Uppark House, then round and on in the direction of Treyford – caught sight of a hawfinch; a lovely bird. Quite warm out of the wind; breezy on top of the hill; beautiful clear day – deep blue sky with fluffy white clouds.

22nd September – [Chalton, Hampshire.] Went to Idsworth, Woodcroft Farm – walked up old lane: picked a small harvest of blackberries: found some mushrooms. Saw in a field by the farm, Mike Millington's two Shire horses – Blossom, and Prince. Lovely sunny day.

16th October – [The 1987 – Hurricane.] The hurricane arrived with 108 m.p.h winds during the night: the hurricane swept through the the whole of the South Coast of England: devastation everywhere. All our lovely walks gone: woods are destroyed – beautiful trees down everywhere. No electric, no phones, or trains. Everything has stopped: no work either – never seen anything like it before. Priory Park – trees are down. The boats in the harbour [Chichester, and Emsworth] many are wrecked. Brighton cut off completely. Chichester, and all the roads around Funtington, and West Ashling, are blocked by fallen trees and debris.

17th October – [Hurricane damage.] Drove to Bosham. Many boats damaged, large yachts and cruisers written off. Walked up to the old stables [Watergate House] and Haslets Copse. Many beautiful trees gone – the old avenue of trees is no more. Ancient flint summer house at Watergate House, is flattened – a sad sight. Stansted woods caught the hurricane badly, with many of the very old trees obliterated. Took numerous storm photographs.

18th October – [Hurricane damage.] Went to Harting, quite a number of trees down. Made our way back through North Marden and Stoughton – Grevatt's Copse is devastated. Some of the most beautiful walks in the area are gone.

25th October – [Hurricane damage.] Drove over to the stables lane, and walked up past Watergate House, [Compton.] Got as far as the avenue of trees – but our way was blocked. Fallen trees along the whole length of the lane block the path. Made our way over to South Holt Farm, where we found only a couple of trees down here. The copse by the old lime kiln devastated – It's a terrible sight when you go for a walk, the countryside is ruined.

27th December – [Treyford.] Went over to Treyford. The 'Wayfarers Post' which used to stand on top of Treyford Hill, for traveller's, has been restored and now stands by the roadside at Treyford. Went into Didling church, beautiful little place of worship; still lit by candlelight – has medieval pews. Weather was dull but mild.

31ˢᵗ December – [Treyford.] Went for a nice walk. It was sunny and quite mild for the time of year – the air fresh and sweet, the day was beautiful. From The Royal Oak, at Hooksway, we roamed to the top of Didling hill. Lots of lovely beech trees along the lane blown down. Came back across the fields. A lovely airing. Walked from Hooksway, to the Devils Jumps, – just past Monkton House. I took several photos of the views. It was sad to see the vast number of wonderfully mature trees, wiped from the landscape by the violent storm of some months past. One wonders how long it will take to clear the debris.

1988

3rd January:- [Compton.] A wet and windy night; still gusty: but the day turned out sunny to good. We started our walk from Compton, at the ruined stables – struggled through the decimated woods, but found the going impossible – so had to take the field route in a circular towards Stoughton. With so many trees down, the woodlands are now, quite impossible to walk through. We spied no wildlife other than a robin; a few blackbirds and some stray rooks.

10th January:- [Stoughton.] Dull, dreary; foggy day. Went over to Walderton, from where we walked up through Lordington Copse, then along Monarch's Way, towards Compton – then circled round the old deer wood and back. Saw several deer; three squirrel's; yellow hammers and the odd blackbird or two: Sue gathered some catkins. The storm devastation wherever we go is terrible: the worst is, that no fallen trees have yet been cleared from the woodlands.

17th January:- [Harting.] Very dense fog along coast. Made our way over to Harting – where, from the summit of Harting Down, a layer of wispy fog appeared like a milky sea over the flat landscape – the village of Harting below us, being just visible – while, the top of the hill opened out to a clear blue sky. We walked for some way along the downs, then headed back down into a valley, where we noticed several warblers; a bullfinch, and a couple of hawks.

24th January:- [Cocking.] Weather; fine and dry today; with the sun making a rare appearance. We went to Cocking, and trekked up along the South Downs Way, past the old farm, and on towards Hooksway. A most beautiful walk – we had a picnic in the woods, on the south side of the hill – Sue picked some catkins. The air was fresh, wonderfully quite: breathtaking scenery. The storm damage, was not a pretty site – never-the-less, a lovely day.

30th January – [Stoughton.] Weather sunny, occasional rain. Went over to Stansted, where we saw about a dozen deer close to the road, the albino was amongst them – pleased to see she still survives. Walked over towards Marden, then cut through to Stoughton. It was heartening to see the trees are now being cleared. We tramped on to Inholmes Wood, to where I had taken a photo a couple of years ago: it is now, almost levelled to the ground. The foresters are now busy clearing the woodlands: I intend to photograph these locations again, to illustrate the change in our countryside since the storm.

31st January – [Cocking.] Beautiful sunny day: wind was chilly. Went over to Cocking, where we walked up along the South Down's Way, towards Hooksway. As we neared the top, we branched off left, then circled round through the coniferous woods. All so quite and peaceful: several deer alarmed by our approach. We sat on a log and had some soup from our flask, followed by a couple of chocolate rolls. Then set off downhill, where we suddenly came to the southern entrance of the disused, Midhurst to Chichester railway tunnel. I climbed down to investigate. The massive, rusting iron doors were open – I could clearly see the half mile distance to the other end. Water was seeping down through the brick archway. I climbed back up the bank with some difficulty. Resolve to bring a torch one day, so I can walk the length of it.

6th February – [West Dean – West Sussex.] Sunny, but cold. We made the most of the day, by going over to West Dean. Walked from the village and along by the river, going southwards; then on to the old disused railway track – on up the hill to a chalk incline – here, we swung off, and up to the summit – towards the Trundle. The path edged down beside the boundary of West Dean House: the richest green moss I had ever seen, growing in abundance on the old flint wall that flanked the property. When we got back down to the foot of the escarpment, I photographed a tiny bridge which spans the river Lavant: wonderful reflections of a farmhouse in the puddles that swamped the lane. A most enjoyable walk.

7th February – [Treyford.] Sunny day. We went over to Treyford and began our walk from Manor Farm. The birds were singing joyfully; rooks adding their homely sounds to this early, Spring day. We climbed the steep, exhausting hill to the summit, then stopped for lunch: much needed tea and cheese rolls. This done, we walked on a short distance, then circled round and back down, soon descending into an old wood, where here, in Elsted Hanger, we found a natural spring, which forms a beautiful waterfall – the very start of a river that winds a course down through the valley – like a tropical garden full of ferns – all so wild, as if never before touched, or seen by a living soul. Beautiful views over the hills. We spied a woodcock in this lovely old wood. Another day of peace, quiet and beauty.

20th March – [West Dean, West Sussex.] We went to West Dean woods – the daffodil wood, [Newfarm Plantation.] where we discovered the ruins of an old cottage. All badly hit by the October storm. The wood-men have cleared quiet a lot of the debris. I suspect, there must be 50 to 80 acres of woodland gone. The daffodils were out in full bloom, lovely sight to see.

30th April – [Sussex / Hampshire border] Went over to Idsworth for a walk – we took a route up past Ditcham Park school, then on in a circular through the woods. Found hoards of orchids, primroses, violets, cowslips, ox-slips and bluebells. A wonderful ramble with all kinds of nature.

2nd May – [Chalton, Hampshire.] Went over to Idsworth again; saw a pair of yellowhammers and a chaffinch in the hedge – which I photographed. We then walked up the old path towards Chaters Well: numerous early purple orchids, primroses and violets all along the way. We later heard the cuckoo for the first time this year. Chaters Well was swarming with thousands of tadpoles. A wonderfully peaceful spring day.

7th May – [Chalton, Hampshire.] Took a walk this evening, round Idsworth: saw a number of rabbits and their young. There appears to be quite a number of yellowhammers this year. Spotted a rabbit with myxomatosis. Later, we saw a tawny owl on the branch of a tree – no more than a few feet away.

8th May – [Stoughton.] Went out about nine O,clock this mor'n: a most beautiful hot day – just like mid-summer! We went over to Walderton: walked up our old lane [Monarch's Way] and in through the woods: a carpet of bluebells. Spotted a deer – was pretty close to us – it stood still for some minutes. Saw a squirrel; some wood warblers, and also a marsh tit – the old copse was teaming with birds and animals.

13th August – [Petworth.] Drove to Fox Hill, and walked down Blackbrook Lane, to the entrance of Westlands Farm. There, we gazed down onto the farmstead – and what a wonderfully old fashioned picture it made – still looking now, as it did when I knew it back in my teenage years. Old Algie Moss, [the farmer – the late Algie Moss] always stuck to the old ways of farming. He always cut the corn with a binder, stooked the sheaves in the field, and thrashed the corn with a great thrashing machine. We wandered on down the lane to Medhone Farm, then turned back towards Blackbrook Farm – a most pleasant walk – peaceful day.

10th September – [Fishbourne.] Beautiful, warm sunny day. Went to Fishbourne and walked along the path to the old cottage which appears to be undergoing renovation. Came to Hook Farm: there, just beyond, we had a picnic on the beach. Strolled along the shore and found a lovely spot in an ancient wood. On the way home we saw eight herons in a field, and a hawk, lots of butterflies about. Spotted a hot air balloon in distance.

1989

2nd January – Went over to Elsted for a walk. We set off from the church and carried on down the right hand path. It was cold and overcast, but dry. Along the way we spotted a common snipe out on the flat marshy land – saw too, a robin and a tiny wren in the hedgerow. Made tracks back to the car and drove over to Turkey Island [Harting] where we walked down a shady lane, which eventually led to an old farm, and an ancient house with a sagging roof and tall chimneys, that leaned unevenly to the wind, like tired old men. The sun came out as we wandered back to the car.

14th January – Went over to Wisborough Green, where we set off on a walk along the old canal route [Wey & Arun canal] a most lovely ramble, full of wildlife – saw a heron, and some guillemots – and teams of rabbits. Weather was sunny and quite warm.

25th March – Drove over to Northchapel – turned off into the old lane that leads down to Pheasant Court Farm: parked up in Chafold wood. There we wandered up along the path and on through Wet Wood – saw a brimstone butterfly – bluebells are out in all their glory; wood anemones blooming too – a most peaceful walk today.

26th March – Went over to Lurgashall and walked up Mill Farm lane. From the farm we turned off onto the footpath that leads on down by the river – we wandered for a mile or two in sublime peace – spotted along the way, a beautiful kingfisher darting along the river – a wisp of tempered blue – gone in a flash. Hoards of primroses along the banks; some with white petals – haven't seen so many for years. Later, we sat on an old log in the warm sun, and there lingered for some long time, listening to the birds singing – and soaking up the glorious day.

7th May – Today we went over to Ebernoe, where we walked down to the pond, and in through the woods – saw an adder. Later, we drove over to Lurgashall, and wandered up the old lane towards Mill Farm – heard the nightingale and the cuckoo – we sat in the sun – a beautiful warm sunny day – the birds sing lovely.

1990

4th March – Drove over to Lurgashall, and walked up the old lane to Mill Farm, then carried on towards the woods: [Dirty Bridge Field woodland] – primroses are out; catkins and pussy-willow hang in clusters. As we made our way round the edge of the lake, [River Park Farm lake] we spotted a couple of deer: lots of fishermen out there. Saw some lapwings in a ploughed field. Tramped on towards the old barns; [Lodge Farm] where close by, we stopped and had a sandwich by the electric pylon – not the most pleasant place to eat, but shaded from the wind. The old barns, which I photographed some time ago, are still intact, though a few tiles have been blown off. Wild daffodils by the stone 'packhorse' bridge: hoards of snowdrops on the river bank – though sadly, they have all gone over. We wandered back through the swampy path that follows the river – a wonderful walk, full of wild spring flowers. A lovely sunny day, warm when shielded from the wind.

17th March – Drove over to Lurgashall, and took a walk up the old lane [Mill Farm lane] and around the lake – clusters of primroses and wild daffodils, with patches of violets and lady's-smock all about here. I took a few photos of some Aylesbury ducks and Brent geese. Lambs about on the farm, and several calves. The weather was warm and sunny, although cloudy at times.

18th March – Went over to Charlton, [Singleton] and walked up the lane [North Lane] to the Downs; the dome of the hills a carpet of cowslips. We wandered on and into woods; [Wellhanger Copse] and there, sat for ages in the sun. Lots of brimstone butterflies, and meadow browns skipping about in this natural sun-trap – the birds singing beautifully – the woodland paths laden with primroses, violets, and lady's-smock: the trees and bushes weighed down with catkins and sweet smelling blossom. A beautifully warm sunny day – all so wonderfully peaceful.

31st March – [West Grinstead.] Today we went over to Dial Post: drove down Swallows Lane and stopped outside 'Cherry Tree Cottage'. Then made our way down to the river, where we had a picnic. This done, we set off on a circular walk, starting from the Shipley road. Took the path that leads up by Honeypools Barn – found along the way, bunches of bluebells, primroses, violets, wood anemones, and ladies smock: it was very warm as we walked. We found a sun trap by a very old packhorse bridge (which I photographed) and sat for about half an hour. A most beautiful peaceful day.

1st April – [Hampshire.] Decided to tread some new ground today – so went over towards Warnford, just past West Meon (Hants). We parked in the woods and had lunch, then walked up a pretty lane and through an orchard, where we found bunches of primroses and violets: saw a deer too. We wandered up past Bere Farm; which has a beautiful old house, (being renovated) with a very old water wheel, that looks similar to the one at 'Carisbrooke Castle', on the Isle of Wight. Outbuildings are very old too, with a granary in the garden. We followed the footpath on and through a couple of fields, which brought us out to the village of Warnford; where flows the River Meon, with its watercress beds: a most beautiful hamlet, full of thatched cottages. From here, we wandered on up to the crest of the downs, and there sat and sipped hot tea from our flask. Can see for miles from this point – easily to as far as Winchester Hill and Beacon Hill. Saw several hares today, and some deer in the fields – one particular piece of open ground, had an abundance of hares – wonderful to see so many all in one place. We found hoards of bluebells, primroses, violets and lady's-smock, on our route back along the lanes to the car at Bere Farm. From here we drove on towards the site of the medieval village of 'Lomer' and Beacon Hill; then into the village of Exton. Doubled back up the hill – then on, and over Winchester Hill – where there was a great flock of sheep with their lambs. I could not resist stopping to take a few photos: lovely to see them all running and skipping about – full of the joys of spring. The weather was warm and sunny, although not as warm as yesterday.

22nd April – Drove over to Elsted, from where we set off along the lane towards the Downs. An exhaustive climb, up and over Treyford Hill, to the 242ft high beacon – stunning views from here, looking down over Harting. Wet and slippery going back. On our way down, we found in the woods, the remnants of an old shed in which was clearly visible, some pumping equipment – what on earth was it used for? I wondered. A profusion of bluebells and violets in and around these ancient woodlands.

28th April – Drove over to Didling. Sat in the field opposite the church and had lunch: watched the rabbits feeding along the lane for some little time – most amusing. We then drove over to Elsted and walked up the stony-path, towards the downs. At the foot of the hills, we branched off to the right. [near Knightsfield.] Carried on for some distance, until we came out of the woods, near East Harting. From here we strayed off the trail and skirted along the edge of the fields: followed some deer tracks through a spinney; where there we found hundreds of early purple orchids. Came out onto open downland [near Down Place] at the bottom of Harting Hill: here, we stepped back onto the footpath – all covered in cowslips and violets: found too, some tiny forget-me-nots up on the downs. Climbed up and over Beacon Hill; then tramped on for some distance on the lower path where, along the way, we spotted an adder, basking in the sun on a huge slab of masonry, that was half hidden in the undergrowth. It was I believe, the largest adder that I had ever seen – so took several photos of it. We then wandered on down the lane and back to car – noting as we went, the numerous flowers we had seen – bluebells; self heal; bugle; white and red dead nettle; yellow archangel; hedge bedstraw; vetch; wood spurge; and stitchwort.

Drove back to Didling, and there sat and watched the rabbits – took several photos. We stayed about half an hour, then drove on home. While driving back through Treyford, we spotted some corn marigolds on a grass bank, which I photographed. Weather was sunny, but wind was very cold on top of hills. We saw a hawk on Harting Down; also chaffinches; bullfinches and wagtails. We also heard the cuckoo up on the hills.

29th April – [Northchapel] We went over to Pheasant Court Farm today, parked up near the lake, [Chaffold Copse lake] which has now been planted, we noticed, with irises. Ambled on through the woods [Wet Wood] and past the old cottage, then out onto the lane, [near Peacock's Farm] and up towards Frith Lodge – the woods are full of bluebells, stitchwort and orchids. We wandered on over to 'Shillinglee' lake; where there, on the bank we sat and sunbathed. Watched for ages the antics of the grebes and the tranquil gliding of geese out on the water; and too, the occasional glimpse of the reed warblers close by. A lovely hot, summers day – we skirted around the lake – an abiding peace: found hoards of bluebells. After a long while, we made tracks back through the fields, past Mitchell Park Farm; and through woods full of bluebells and whitebells to Freehold Farm. There we came upon the old farmer [David Burden] tending his lambs – we passed the time of the day with him: chatting about the old farmhouse, and of farming in the olden days. He told us that he had read Barclay Wills book; and that he knows quiet a few relatives of the old shepherds mentioned by that author. As we carried on our way, we saw a couple of hot air balloons, that drifted over towards Northchapel. Lovely day, warm, relaxing very enjoyable: we heard the cuckoo while walking up by Freehold Farm.

5th May – [Eartham] Today, Sue and I have been together for 20 years; and the weather on that first date was then, as it is now – a most beautiful hot sunny day. We drove to the top of Goodwood, then made our way over towards Eartham; where we took a walk through the woodlands. Found an old barn and a pond – no flowers, all very barren. We did find however, an old kiln in the woods either a lime burner or charcoal. We also saw a tiny squirrel; he couldn't have been out of the dray for very long, he was lovely.

6th May – Today we drove to Patching, and took a walk over the downland and on through woodland paths for about a mile. Then we came out again onto the open downs; were there, we found hundreds of cowslips. We met a fellow walker, who, like us, loves to wander about the countryside – she tells us she has done a lot of walking over by Didling, Treyford and Harting. We chatted for a few minutes, then tramped on – all was quiet, uninterrupted peace for another mile – then, suddenly, that silence was broken by the screeching of a terrified beast. We swung round, and were amazed to see, further up the hill, a weasel chasing a rabbit – a rare sight to witness. So there we stood motionless, watching this wretched animal racing for its life – the chase went on for some five minutes, after which, the bunny, we were pleased to note, managed to escape. Walked back through a tree plantation. Weather is very hot. Lovely red sunset. Found some borage. (herb)

7th **May** – Bank holiday – [Treyford] Weather cooler today. We went over to Didling and parked at the church. Climbed up the hill to the stile, then wandered off along the edge of the fields looking for fossils: found a strangely shaped, gnarled log, which we took back to the car for varnishing at home. We then drove to Bepton and walked up the road, to as far as the tiny thatched cottage by the T junction. Here, we turned into the shaded lane, that goes on up the hill to Bepton Down – spotted a deer as we made our way along this secluded path. High up on the hillside we found a spot shaded from the wind – and there we sat in the warmth of the sun – an ideal place to eat our sandwiches. Found all about us, hoards of cowslips: there were too, lots of butterflies – orange tips; blues; brimstones and fritillaries; small coppers, and woody browns. We lazed in the sun for about an hour: saw pheasants and rabbits: bunches of campion about here also. Our midday lunch done – we sauntered back down the track, and then drove to Cocking. Parked up, and set off along the old quarryman's path, that leads up to the chalk-pit – once there, we hunted for fossils – but to no avail. Though we did notice, about 50ft up, an old lime kiln perched on the face of the quarry. Weather in the afternoon clouded over; much cooler than of late, but still warm, if out of the wind. We have caught the sun today. Saw some early purple orchids, up along the Bepton lane; and in the quarry; also ox-eye daisies.

12th **May** – [Sussex / Hampshire, border.] We went over to Deanlane End this morning – pulled into the lay-by outside of Diddybones Knap, cottage, and there we brought some wild flowers – evening primroses; field scabious, and meadow cranesbill. The lady tells us, she started selling them, when her hobby grew too big. We'll plant them near our pond. We then drove on up by Woodgate Farm, and there noticed that Mike Millington, (farmer) has a foal – a tiny 'Shire' – in his field; his two heavy horses, Prince and Beauty are still there. We carried on over to Hooksway and parked in the Royal Oak car park. The pub, although very old, has a modern extension. From here, we walked up the lane past the old house, [Philliswood Farm] which was once a beautiful old dwelling with flagstone floors; an orchard, and a well in the garden. The house has now been modernised, and consequently, lost its old world charm. We trudged on up towards Buriton Farm. This little used path is covered with early purple orchids, and cowslips; also stitch wort; white and pink campion; bladder campion; buttercups; yellow archangel; silverweed; birds foot trefoil; tufted vetch; herb robert; chalk milkwort; woodruff; forget-me-nots, and self heal. The old Buriton Farm, farmhouse has, standing by the front gate, a six-foot high, 'crudely-made' wooden man – a representation of St Christopher, the patron saint of wayfarers – with an infant, just as artistically constructed, sitting on his shoulders. The owner [the late Mrs Woods] tells us that they have lived there for about 30 years: the house has no electric, and no running water. They say that, as the place lays in a deep crutch of land, high up on the downs, between Didling and Harting Hill, it is sometimes completely cut off in the winter. There is, hanging on a front elevation of the house, numerous artefacts which have been dug up from the garden over the years: other parts of the building are covered in clematis - it always looks so very peaceful. We tramped on up the track and took the right hand fork – we've never been that way before – a lovely old route to ramble along. But after a while, we came back and continued up our usual way. The ancient oak tree, that we have passed so many times before, has died; a sad loss, we will miss it – it was all part of the beauty of the landscape that we have come to love so much over the years. We carried on up the trail – the banks and fields covered in cowslips: we saw a green woodpecker in the grass. Went on up towards Telegraph Hill – found some milkwort up there. Made our way back down to Hooksway, where at bottom of the lane, there was a field covered in cowslips; although they are nearly all over – must remember this, so I can get a photograph of them next year. Weather today was quite sunny and warm; although not as hot as last week.

20th May – We went over to Hooksway and parked at pub. Walked up to the top lane, towards Buriton Farm – soon turning left onto a footpath we hadn't been on before. Traipsed back through West Dean Estate woods: they've cleared all the trees, and made several access routes. Wandered back through the estate – sat and had picnic in a field. We then climbed to the top of Harting Hill, then down again to Telegraph House, and back to Hooksway. There we decided to do another small walk through the woodlands. Weather was warm and sunny – we saw no wildlife: too many people about. Spotted the tail end of a grass snake on our way back to car.

2nd June – We went to a fête at Lurgashall. They had a bric-a-brac stall: brought a silver bangle, and a flower press; also a book on fossils and some other bits – cheese from the farm at Gospel Green, and some duck eggs. After leaving the fête we drove towards Kirdford – the old houses outside the apple farm, are being renovated. We found meadows full of ox eye daisies, a beautiful sight in these days of sterile fields – so often full of nothing but grass. Drove down the road – our sudden appearance frightened a deer – we eventually came out at Hawkhurst Court. On our way home – just past Noah's Farm Yard (Grittenham Farm) a weasel ran out in front of the car.

9th June – [Kirdford] We drove to Strood Green near Wisborough Green, and parked opposite the road that goes to Hawkhurst Court. Set off on our walk through fields of ox-eye daisies; then in through the woods, crossed the lane and came out by Crimbourne Farm: [which I photographed] most picturesque, with lovely old barns and outbuildings – all set within its own woodlands. The place appears as if it's not being lived in, at this present moment in time. We wandered on up through Hawkhurst Court, which used to be the local manor house – all the farm and estate houses, have now been converted into private homes. There is a large lily filled lake, at the bottom of the garden – a most beautiful place to live. Walked on up the hill and sat on a tree stump; and there, we hungrily dug into our sandwiches. Our midday break done, we continued through the woods, coming soon to a lovely old fashioned meadow full of hundreds of orchids – took several photos. It was here, that we met a chap who was looking for butterfly orchids: he told us where he'd found several different species of these beautiful flowers, and the time of year to find them – he certainly knew his hobby. He took us through the 'Cuts' and showed us two white butterfly orchids – absolutely lovely – well worth the walk. On our way through to the Cuts, he told us where to find bee orchids on Harting Down: also purple helleborine; which can be found in the 'Cuts' in late August, and in early September – he's also seen there, fly-orchids, and man-orchids. He gave us his phone number, in case we spot a rare specimen.

The weather was quite warm, walking. We saw several rabbits; a little owl flying through the woods; a deer, and a woodpecker. When we where in the woods, on the other side of the road, we spotted a stag bolting through the jungle of trees – just caught a glimpse of his red coat.

10th June – Today, we drove over to Ebernoe – hunting for orchids to photograph. The green winged orchids, are over, so we drove to the 'Mens'. Set off up the hill – where we spotted a fox trotting along the middle of the path – his lovely red coat stood out in the green lane – a beautiful sight. Turned left and ended up back on the road – about 100 yards from where we had started! Went back up the hill, and eventually found the track to the meadow that we had discovered the other day – and there we sat and had lunch. Found a dead adder – not far from where we had been sitting. This meadow is full of spotted-orchids: not sure if the white ones we found are the 'lesser-butterfly' orchids or not. Went through a quaint little wicket gate in the second meadow, and over an old packhorse bridge – very old – could be medieval; the bricks were tiny. Some Solomon's seal on banks of a stream. This field will be lovely next month. Just up the path from the bridge, is an old cottage with a duck pond – well geese – beehives and roses round the door. Saw a newt in the grass, nearly managed to pick him up – but he got away. Walked back through woods: found some monkshood – came out onto a byroad, full of large private houses – traipsed on up to top of the lane; but had to retrace our steps to find the right route. Saw another fox, strolling along, as if without a care – he was quite unaware that we were sneaking up behind him – but he suddenly cut into the woods and was gone. We came out at Brickiln Dairies – a most beautiful cottage, with monkshood; poppies; columbine; daisies and all kinds of flowers in the garden. We crossed over the road and wandered up along a trail which was not frequently used: found some yellow loosestrife – then came to a better used track, which led into a most beautiful meadow – full of spotted-orchids; ox- eye-daisies; roses, and honeysuckle; with rabbits playing in the grass: we saw several jays. Carried on up to the end of the lane, where an old cottage, with shutters that had hearts carved into them, overlooked the meadowland. From here, we doubled back into woods, and returned to Crimbourne Farm. Lovely long walk – and we've seen plenty of wildlife and rare flowers. Took photo of marsh-orchids as we came out of last field. We also saw a frog jump into one of the streams which run through the 'Mens'.

30th June – We went to see Nigel [the celebrated Chichester artist – the late, Nigel Purchase] in the morning, regarding an article I have for the Heritage magazine: also, one of my photos, which is in the latest edition. We drove over to Harting, parked at the foot of the hill, and then set off in search of bee-orchids. Just as we got through a farm gate we saw two foxes; a dog and vixen: the latter ran back, stopped and looked at us for about a minute, then darted into the bushes. We wandered on up to the highest point of the hill, and there collapsed for rest – hundreds of marbled whites on the downland; and numerous swallows too. From here, we went down the path towards the Mardens – where there, along the way, there were hundreds of rabbits. We slipped silently onto a private trail – but found new fencing has just been erected – so traipsed back and sat on a couple of lifeless ant hills; now all covered in thyme. How lovely it must have been, over fifty years ago, when the downs had gone untouched by the plough for hundreds of years! Lots of empty snail shells about here. We followed some animal tracks – hoping to see the foxes again – but to no avail; only rabbits running for dear life down the hills. It was a very clear sunny day – but windy. You could see for miles all around. The telegraph poles on Harting down, have had the cables taken out and laid underground – lets us hope the poles come down too, soon. The landscape along the valley, will then be uncluttered once more. Got back to car without finding any orchids; except along the banks at the side of the lane; but they where only the common spotted species.

1991

4th January – [Stoughton] Went for a walk in the afternoon, up by the old woodsman's cottage. Wandered through the woods, [Lordington Copse] where we spotted about 8 deer, and quite a few squirrel's: listened to a blackbird singing. The old shepherds hut is still in the rough meadow – I took some photos of it. We crossed the road and roamed round the fields – then made our way back to the car and home. Weather was dull in morning, cleared up in afternoon; it was quite sunny until about four o'clock, when it rained.

12th January – [Fishbourne.] Another visit to Fishbourne. We walked down to the remains of the old salt mill in the late afternoon sun. There were multitudes of sea birds about the mud flats. As it was low tide, we tramped from the ruined mill, up along the hard towards Dell Quay. Most beautiful sunset. They forecast a stiff frost tomorrow.

13th January – [Duncton.] This afternoon we went over to Duncton Mill Farm: the old Mill Farm has, during the past fifty years, been altered beyond recognition. The millpond appears to flow from a natural spring. We wandered on up the lane towards the Petworth road. Nearby, there is a lovely house which has a stream running through the garden, with woods all around. A squirrel in the garden kept stealing from the bird table; we laughed at his antics. Kept on up the footpath, and so along by an old orchard, which had several trees laden with mistletoe. From here, we carried on over to Barlavington, where we found an abundance of primroses, and celandines: caught site of a piebald blackbird, and spotted in the distance, a small herd of deer bolting across the fields. There is a lovely old yew tree by the farm; exceedingly old. The tiny church is quaint, and very peaceful – most picturesque – I took several photos of it. Walked back to car along the old lane; where along this route, stands a very ancient cottage – 14th or 15th century – the front elevation bowed with age. Weather today has been beautiful; very cold, but sunny; haw frost hung about all day. A glorious evening, with a golden sunset, which cast long, deep shadows from the smallest mounds in the fields.

19th January – [Nr Harting] This afternoon we drove over to Treyford, where we went for a walk down by the beautiful old stream in the valley. Very ancient packhorse bridge spans the stream – I took several photos of the landscape and the bridge. We saw robins, wrens, thrushes, blackbirds; listened to the rooks cawing in the rookery close by the river. One of the most beautiful, old fashioned places in Sussex. Made our way home – turned up road towards old stables – at West Marden, we saw a herd of deer in the fields, with an albino amongst them – which I photographed. Snowdrops just starting to come out at Stansted. Sun went down red – stunningly beautiful.

1st February – [Stoughton.] This afternoon we went over to Stansted for a walk: snowdrops are out; though not anywhere near as many as there once was. The great storm of '87 has taken many of the trees from the area, and the woodsmen have cleared the debris – which seems to have caused some damage to the snowdrops. We drove on over to Forestside, and walked up the lane towards the old ruined lime kiln: the sun was beautiful, birds were beginning to sing. Robins, wrens, thrush, blackbirds: rabbits in the distant fields. I took some photos of free range chickens, with the old cottage in the background. We wandered on down to the long meadow, then made our way back up along the side of the ancient field. The air was crisp – the sun warm. Weather came out sunny by mid morning and remained lovely all day.

3rd February – Woke to a severe frost this morning. Made up a picnic, then drove over to North Marden: Parked at a field gate – had lunch in car, and then drove down to the arched lodge. Walked along footpath to fields, then stepped over an electric fence to go into the woods, [Edger Plantation] very quiet at the moment, not many birds about. Walked up paths where, along the way, we found a spent bullet shell, looked like a 303 mm – the type they use for killing deer; decided to get out of the woods as soon as possible. No flowers about yet; although there will be lots of foxgloves later. Wandered on along the path, where soon we came to a couple of large trees blown down in the [87] storm; the roots were so large it was like a little cave inside. The old shepherds hut is still there; although going to rack and ruin very quickly.

Traipsed back to car – a lovely walk, very enjoyable – felt refreshed, although tired. Came back through Up Marden and along lanes – drove up past the Woodmans Cottage to Stansted – where we stopped to look at the snowdrops. Weather frosty and cold – but sunny. Saw a deer and a squirrel.

9th February – Very cold again this morning – although, no more snow. This afternoon we drove over to Compton: had quiet a snowstorm when we got to Stoughton – I took several photographs. There were quiet a few people sledging on Compton Hill. While out driving we saw lots of birds: a poor little thrush sitting by the roadside, looked frozen. There were flocks of pigeons; some robins; a yellow hammer; blackbirds; and pheasants; also a squirrel and droves of rabbits. Weather still bitterly cold, frost and snow.

17th February – [Ebernoe.] We walked from Balls Cross, up the old lane, past High Buildings Farm, and on towards Ebernoe Common. As we got deeper into the woodlands, the track we were on, suddenly petered out; and before we realised it, we were lost. We scampered on through the thickets for some good long way – coming eventually out onto a path: this we followed until we came unexpectedly, out onto the road that leads to Ebernoe. Having got our bearings – we made our way back through the common, towards Balls Cross – then we slipped off the track again. Kept on going, until we eventually came out onto a rough piece of meadowland. There, we found a number of crumbling flint walls: [the ruins of Old House Farm, Balls Cross] the whole area was littered with rusting farm machinery – the remains of an old binder, and the remnants of a corn drill. There was too, many old bottles and broken pots and an old kettle; a nearly complete, old iron bed, fully intact with brass knobs – clearly, this was the ruins of an old farmstead. A most interesting walk – though we did not see much nature today. The weather a bit dull all day, but the sun eventually came out, it turned cold about 3ish. Lovely sunset.

28th February – [Stoughton.] The sun being out, we went over to Stansted for a walk through the woods – the sweet scented snowdrops are out in full bloom – I took several photos. The birds were in fine chorus, as we wandered through a spinney – the catkins hung in clusters. We sat resting on an old log – clutching our hot mug of tea, fresh from the flask – it was lovely to sit and listen to the birds singing. Weather was mild, with long sunny periods.

23rd March – [Petworth.] Went into the park – and from there, we crossed the road and took the footpath that goes up by Limbo Farm, and over towards Keyfox Farm. Some beautiful countryside over that way – with blankets of wild daffodils in the woods. We saw several deer; some rabbits; squirrel's, and various woodland birds. Happily, the old woodlands about this patch of land, appeared untouched by the '87 storm. Weather was bright and sunny first thing, but clouded over and remained so until about half past three, when it suddenly brightened up again. On our way home in the evening we looked on in wonder, as the sun slipped gloriously crimson, beyond the downs.

24th March – [Ebernoe.] Went to Balls Cross, for a walk. The rooks nesting in the lane by the entrance to High Buildings, squabbled incessantly; their neighbours, constantly thieving the best nesting twigs high up in the rookery. We stood and listened to them – always a homely sound at any time of the year. Here we saw a weasel – he poked his head through the hedge and looked up at us! We saw too, a wonderful little field-mouse. We set off up the lane on our walk – soon cutting across the meadows, which where laden with primroses, cowslips, violets; and there were too, signs of early purple orchids. As we wandered through the woods, we spotted a beautiful red fox, which scurried away on seeing us. We came out of the woodlands and cut across the meadow towards Palfrey Farm: it was lovely to hear the chorus of skylarks overhead; and to see so many rabbits and pheasants along the way. Daffodils in some of the copses were quite numerous: the adders were up and about; we noticed one lazily basking in the sun beside the footpath. We stood and watched it for a while, until it became aware of our presence and slid off into the undergrowth. At last, we circled round and made our way back to Balls Cross. Weather:- sunny periods all day.

30th March – [Petworth.] We set off up Blackbrook Lane, to the entrance of Westlands Farm – where there, we heard the unmistakeable sound of pee-wits crying across the fields. From here, we turned off the path, and made a large circular route, through Holland Wood, seeing hoards of wildlife along the way. We wandered through clusters of daffodils, violets and periwinkles; their intoxicating scents, being a lure for the giant bumble bees that hovered in droves around the wild flowers. The hooting of an owl echoed through the woods; rabbits played in the fields; deer grazed in the sun, and butterflies were out and about: the red admiral, brimstone and wooded brown. Saw a nuthatch and a green woodpecker: primroses all out along the hedgerow banks. Our quiet walk disturbed an old bitch fox, who scurried off into the copse; and a stoat darted across the footpath: pheasants were in droves. Amongst the periwinkles that we saw in the woods earlier, there was one which was all white, except for one petal which was purple. Weather – sunny and warm all day.

31st March – [Kirdford.] Went over to the 'Mens', and walked through the woods close to Hawkhurst Court, then around an ancient meadow – host to numerous wild flowers, all growing in the mossy grass. There were primroses, white and purple violets; cowslips; ox-slips; daffodils; wild strawberries; lords & ladies; celandines; ladies-smock, and orchids – not yet out in bloom. We also saw a squirrel – and there was too, a thrush sitting on her nest. This very ancient meadow, I believe must be one of the most important areas of natural history to be found in Sussex. One can only hope it remains untouched in every meaning of the way. Weather:- cloudy in the morning, with sunny spells in the afternoon, warmish all day.

April 7th – [Petworth.] Went to Coultershaw, and walked up 'Hungers Lane' past Kilsham Farm; over the bridge and on up the lane. A beautiful byway full of primroses – with too, the early signs of carpets of bluebells. The high banks each side of the lane are covered by hazel bushes, which stretch over to form a beautiful arch; a green cloister, that shelters the walker from the midday sun, through the whole length of this ancient highway. Weather: sunny periods, with a very cold wind.

13th April – [Ebernoe.] Went over to Ebernoe church to see if there were any green winged orchids; but unfortunately, none about. The church had been decorated for Easter, with primroses and moss all around the windowsills. We walked through Swedes Copse; which was completely covered with daffodils: I have not before seen, a wood which has such a complete blanket of daffodils. This afternoon we went over to Balls Cross for a walk around the woods and meadows. Went over by the ruins of Old House Farm: many wild flowers: daffodil; primroses; and early purple orchids. Saw a blackcap and heard a cuckoo: a deer; brimstones butterflies; a small blue; comma; and some red admirals. There were also many violets – came across a bouquet of these wonderfully scented flowers growing in the nook of a tree – most unusual: the celandines were out in all their glory:

14th April – Went over to Up Marden, to take another photo of the toothworts we had found in the roadside banks last week! We walked down the old lane by Up Marden church, then back up the steep hill across the field. We then drove over to Didling Hill and parked at the old shepherds church (St. Andrews): walked up the lane and across the fields, heading westwards towards Treyford. Spotted an old fox by the spring pond, which I took a couple of photos of. Lovely day. Weather cloudy at first, but came out bright later. Coldish wind.

18th April – [Compton.] In the afternoon we went to Up Marden, where the roadside banks are covered with a blanket of violets. Some lovely examples of the toothwort – a plant in the orchid group, which is quite rare. Weather:- sunny periods, with a cold wind.

April 20th – Went over towards Petworth to the meadow, near the 'Cuts' – its full of cowslips; lady's smock; primroses and violets – it looks really beautiful and old fashioned. A couple of orchids were out – the meadow is absolutely full of them; but they have yet to come out. It must be one of the rarest fields around – it would be a crime if it where ever ploughed. It started to snow. Drove round through Kirdford, to Northchapel, then near Lurgashall, where the sky looked black and stormy. Drove on home through Midhurst, Duncton and Lavant. Weather warm, when the sun was out; but cold with wintry showers.

21st April – [Kirdford.] Today we went again over to the 'Mens:' walked up to the meadow which was full of cowslips and primroses: saw a green woodpecker and lots of rabbits. As we were coming into the meadow, through the wicket gate we disturbed two deer. Bluebells are coming out in the woods: maybe next week they will be more colourful. Weather sunny periods.

5th **May** – [Fittleworth.] Drove over to Bedham, to look at the old derelict school: I took several photos of the place, then headed back to the car. We were just about to get into it, when a rather bohemian, middle aged fellow, with a beard and hair down to his shoulders, suddenly appeared from the farm opposite. I had to look twice, for his face was daubed with make-up; his fingernails bright red. He walked over to me and asked in soft friendly tones, if I had a cigarette. He then mumbled something about the gypsies stealing tiles from the school; and from the back of the farm. There was something provokingly interesting about him – he was a true English eccentric, and I wanted to know more – we chatted a while. "I'm an artist," he said. "Do come in and have a look at my paintings." We – Sue and I, followed him past the farm barns and in to the oak panelled farmhouse – a slovenly nest, full of throws and old sofas – a great pot of vegetable stew steamed in a copper pot in the kitchen – his dinner by all accounts. He invited us to stay for lunch – I respectfully declined – he held up his paintings: oils on hardboard; a crazy mess of fire and torment, brushed into a human face. And another, much the same – followed by yet more. He spoke, as he passed me his pictures, with a 'well-cultured' accent – he was certainly, highly educated. We made our excuses and headed back out through the farmyard, where there, I noticed a huge dovecote built onto what appeared to be the chassis of a lorry – chickens strutted about the barn door; I swung round and took a few photos of that picturesque scene. Then, in a trice we where gone – heading off up the road in the car. [It has, in recent years, come to my attention from a reliable source, that this elderly fellow has long since left this world – the old farm having been re- let to different tenants.]

29th **June** – Lovely sunny day. Drove to Balls Cross, and went up along the lane into the meadows to look for flowers: lots of honeysuckle and wild roses in hedgerows, but none in fields – slipped into a copse – the footpaths are still very muddy after all the rain. In the woods we found hundreds of orchids: marsh orchids; spotted and lesser butterfly orchids. Haven't seen so many different species of orchids in one place for years

– a truly beautiful sight. We sat in the field, and had lunch – saw a barn owl. Walked back through woodlands, to where there is a caravan in the meadow – saw a deer in the hayfield. Sat for a few minutes in the sun – lovely and peaceful. Picked some honeysuckle, and roses – a wonderfully sweet smelling bunch of summer flowers. Wandered through second meadow and back to car through fields.

As its still lovely and sunny, we decided to drive over to Egdean, to the river – the banks were a mass of orchids – saw some calves at the farm. Sauntered over to the tiny arched bridge. Its crumbling brickwork looks a sorry sight – if it gets any worse they will pull it down, and put up a modern monstrosity. Drove home through Barlavington. Saw lots of rabbits, and a baby squirrel. The sun was starting to look watery.

25th **September** – [Stoughton.] Went to Forestside to take some photos of sloe berries, for the Heritage magazine. Walked down lane, took photos, then carried on to the old cottage, [Warren Down] where we sat on log and had a cup of tea. We lingered there for some while, idly watching the antics of the pheasants and rabbits –. Suddenly, a commotion broke out – a weasel appeared, as if from nowhere, to chase a baby rabbit. The poor thing luckily escaped – but undeterred, the weasel continued on its pursuit for prey – racing after pheasants and anything that moved. Quick as light, it saw another rabbit – chased it; caught it – the scream was horrendous. Continued back up the path, picked blackberries: had lunch at top of the hill at West Marden. Then did circular walk. Sun came out on the way home. Weather dull in morning, sunny in afternoon.

1994

1st January – [Westbourne, West Sussex.] Went over to Racton, and walked up through Racton Park Farm – wonderful old fashioned landscapes. Holly trees are laden with berries. The rooks are busy with their nesting – much squabbling going on – how I love to hear those birds; their cawing always takes my mind back to youthful days. We spotted a couple of yellowhammers. Beautiful day, frosty in the morning.

2nd January – [Lodsworth.] Drove to Lodsworth, parked close to the church. Sunny all day, so we went for a walk down across the old meadow to the river – followed it for a short distance into the woods. Water was running fast and deep, due to the recent heavy rain. Strolled back into Lodsworth and looked around church. Primroses and snowdrops are out in bloom: a monkey puzzle tree in the churchyard. We went and had a look at the grave of E.H. Shepherd, illustrator, of 'Winnie the Pooh' and 'Wind in the Willows' – then we continued on to Half Way Bridge; wandered round and through the hamlet of River and back to Lodsworth.

4th January – [Chichester harbour.] Floods in Sussex are very bad; worst for many years. Bosham; Chidham; Lavant; Singleton and many more villages flooded out. Went this afternoon down to Emsworth, for a walk along the beach. Wind quite cold but dry. Saw an egret, down on the mudflats and a few Brent geese. The recent heavy rains have begun to wash away some of the footpaths along by the shoreline fields.

8th January – We went for a drive over to Stoughton: took photos of the floods – drove on over towards Chichester, and through Lavant, then on to Harting; the floods all along this route being very bad. Helped a woman to restart her Range Rover, which was stranded in the floods on the Lavant to Harting road.

12th January – [Stoughton.] Went to Dean Lane End, which was cut off and very flooded. We had to walk about a mile up the flooded road, and through Idsworth to get to Finchdean, where there was a lot of activity, with the fire engines pumping out people's swamped houses.

15th January – [Chichester.] Went through Chichester on our way to Storrington, took the route over the 'Bailey bridge' that spans the floods by the Chichester Motel. Traffic entering the city was jammed for about 3 miles.

18th June – [Stoughton.] We went over to Racton – walked up the old stony lane to the 'Monument' – an awesome ruin, dizzyingly high – the prospect from the top no doubt, spectacular – but now, impossible to climb to see such sights. It must have been a magnificent building in its day: built by Lord Halifax, in the eighteenth century as a summer retreat – but apparently, used at a later date – "by ladies and gentlemen of ill repute" – compelling Lord Halifax, to order its destruction – after which, it is said to have been used by smugglers to signal ships into Langstone Harbour. Today, the old Folly, is nothing more than a masonry skeleton – its vaulted basement stained with camp-fire soot; the floor, littered with beer cans: – viewed from a distance, the hollow windows and doors, look hauntingly out onto a beautiful, undulating landscape.

28th June – [Lurgashall.] Drove to Lurgashall, where we walked for a couple of miles in the direction of Dial Green. We then circled round towards Lickfold, then back to Lurgashall. Lovely walk; many wild flowers – tufted vetch; honeysuckle; yarrow; betany; knapweed; ox-eye daisies; yellow vetch; dog-rose and burnet rose. As we silently wandered in peace, the sweet breath of the honeysuckle, mingled with that of the hay and cornfields, that were all about us: crickets in the grass made their presence known. The call of a woodpecker caught our attention – we spotted its beautiful green plumage as it took off from a nearby tree and flew across the meadow. May flies were out – incessantly busy, flitting about the hedgerows and fields. As we passed by High Hampstead Farm, I noticed a horseshoe nailed above the door: so the old countryman's superstition still linger on in some remote places.

1997

16th January – [Harting.] Drove over to Turkey Island, where we saw a most beautiful scene in the fields – mist had gathered like a billowy blanket over a meadow, with hedgerows and trees peeping out above, and the field quite clear below – while at the same time, the sun shone brightly all around, lighting up the whole dramatic scene. Half a dozen deer grazed peacefully on the far side of this meadow – a most beautiful picture.

25th January – [East Lavington.] Went for a walk over Lavington Common: early morning mist hung heavy in the pine woods – the sun lanced through the trees most picturesquely – the glory of the first light of day. As we were making our way down a lane, Sue spotted a weasel darting about as they do – looking for prey. We watched him for some minutes, until he disappeared. Then we drove over to South Ambersham, and walked up the lane to the river. Two lovely old ancient bridges span this stream – I took some photo's of them. There was, a few hundred yards further along a heron waiting motionless for his dinner. We wandered further up the lane towards Manor Farm, then on over the meadows.

26th January – [Graffham.] Went over to South Ambersham, again today. The meadows looked beautiful, covered in haw frost, with here and there, a touch of morning mist. We watched the river gliding slow beneath the ancient bridge; listened to the rooks cawing in the distance – a homely sound – a ring of old England. We continued on to Selham, where we wandered on up an old lane, and through a farmyard towards the redundant railway line. The route was, although partly frozen, very muddy in places – we soon returned, not having our wellies on. Went for another walk a little further on up the road; then returned to Ambersham, to take more pictures of the old bridge. The distant hills looked greyish and far away – a sign of good, to fair weather for the next few days.

15th February – [Lodsworth.] Most beautiful day – very springlike. Drove over to Lickfold – walked in a circular from Lickfold pub to Cobden Farm and back. Looked in to a hovel – a small open sided barn – where we saw an owl box; the owl was there, silently sitting. Many old houses of interest about the hamlet of Lickfold, 'The Cottage,' particularly so, as it appears to have a Georgian style manor-house front, with a number of windows blocked up; while the rear of the building is in the style of a beamed cottage. I believe this may have been the house that belonged to Mary Chalcraft, [one of my maternal ancestors] who lived there in the late 17th Century – It is mentioned in her will.

16th February – Wet and windy day. This afternoon, we drove over to Compton [West Sussex] to Littlegreen school, where there is a photographic exhibition being held – there were many pictures of the villagers in the olden days – some going back to as far as the 1840's when photography first began. A most interesting local event.

20th February – [Marden.] Went over to East Marden, where the old well, that stands in the middle of village is being re-thatched. This picturesque construction, that in bygone days, sheltered the villagers from the rain, as they pulled water from the murky depths, was last thatched in 1976. I chatted to the two master thatchers – Paul Cook and Graham Baskery, who told me they were using reed imported from France, it being better quality and more readily available. It seems that almost 70% of thatching reeds are nowadays imported. They said that the job would take less than a week to complete. Its heartening to see good conservation going on in this lovely old village.

21st February – [Compton.] This afternoon, the wind abated a little, and the sun peeped out briefly – prompting a walk over 'Watergate' – Locksash. The snowdrops are out in profusion, and the birds begin to sing – blackbirds especially so. Close to 'Watergate' there is an old tree of curious growth; the trunk having grown up for a couple of feet vertically, then it has taken a sharp right angle, continuing to grow horizontally, with various branches growing vertically from this main trunk. Its appearance is most unusual, yet strangely picturesque. Great patches of velvety moss have, over the years, grown on the horizontal trunk of this tree, which adds to its uniqueness. On this old tree today, I spotted a sparrow hawk, waiting for his prey.

Regarding the unusual growth of trees, there is a particular oak in the area of Elsted, which flanks the road, that has somehow become attached to a holly tree – the two separate species having become the growth of one, coupled together. Another instance that I know of is that of two separate fir trees, located in Petersfield, and situated beside the little stream there. These two trees, although growing about a couple of feet apart, have a branch about three feet from the ground which joins both the separate trunks; they are naturally linked together – like Siamese twins.

4th **March** – Drove to Compton, [West Sussex] turned off towards Locksash, from where I went for a walk up by Watergate Hanger. The low flint wall beside the lane is covered in patches of downy moss and lichens, with clusters of dark green ivy hanging in the most picturesque way. Finches and blackbirds sang beautifully, and the wood pigeons, that are so abundant about here, cooed softly in the distance. I spotted a small herd of deer grazing in a field far away. The rain stopped and the sun struggled through the dense cloud. Then, in the late afternoon, the clouds parted and the sun shone gloriously.

15th **March** – We learned today, that the comet 'Hale-Bopp,' would be visible this evening. Luckily, the night sky was very clear, so we went outside: and yes, there, high in the heavens, we could see it perfectly – most interesting to see the long tail of light that trailed off from it. We used our binoculars; but indeed, it could easily be seen with the naked eye. It apparently passes over every four thousand years.

16th **March** – [Treyford.] Went over to Treyford – where we went for a walk down the path that leads to the little flowing river, then up along the meadows to Newhouse Farm. Turned towards Grevatts, and back along the old lane. Most beautiful walk – could hear lapwings in the distance and that ever English sound of rooks drifting over from their colony – lambs bleating about the meadows – doves cooed and the sun fell warm on our backs: primroses growing down by the gentle flowing stream, where also the hearts-tongue fern grows in clumps.

22nd March – [Tillington.] Decided to go to the Manor of Dean, where the gardens are open today! Most beautiful old place – 16th century – with old mullioned windows. The back entrance, and hallway was open to the public – so I walked into the oak panelled room, where before me was a long refractory table, with six sturdy legs. Pewter plates and pots, jugs and drinking mugs lined the shelves of an ancient dresser, giving the room a most old fashioned feeling. We walked through the gardens amongst hoards of daffodils, tulip trees, hyacinths, and primulas; while the rooks in their nesting colony above us, added to that most peaceful, old world setting. I took a couple of photo's of the house and part of an old arched gate within the garden wall: and too, the walk that cuts down through a most picturesque hazel spinney, lined with daffodils. We met an old lady there, who had travelled especially down from London, to see this unique place. We had a cup of tea in the garden, looking over to the distant downs – the kitchen is oak beamed and typically Sussex. Miss Mitford, who's house it is, is a rather stout, elderly lady – kind; but apparently, she stands no truck! Most enjoyable couple of hours there.

23rd March – [Sutton.] Went over to Glatting Farm: a most beautiful old farm, with lovely old out buildings and barns. Here is the quietest place in West Sussex – no traffic noise, no aircraft noise – peace with only the pleasant sounds of birds – skylarks and finches, with a few rooks cawing in the distance. The lane that leads up to this quaint old farmhouse is flanked by high banks, upon which grow a profusion of celandines, primroses, and white and purple violets. Hazel saplings and blackthorn have sprouted up on a stretch of the route too, which gives a fine show of catkins; pussy willow and May blossom along the hedgerows. At the bottom end of this old sunken lane, a tiny stream glides through grazing meadows, along which, and a little way from the road, a quaint old bridge spans the river. The hedges are beginning to bud, and the moss in vast patches looks rich and green – hearts-tongue ferns add to the splendour of this out of the way place; where the very quietness is a rare joy in these noisy hum-drum days.

28th March – Drove over to South Stoke: breathtaking views – a tiny church steeple in the distance, the red roofs of houses clustered around it – for all the world, a most English scene. Gentle sloping downs –

rooks sailing about in the bluest of skies – the river Arun winding its course through to Amberley, and beyond. Primroses and celandines out in profusion along the banks; with too, bunches of those wonderfully scented purple violets. A glorious day – clear blue sky, with cotton wool clouds that drift about in the most picturesque way – a stunningly beautiful sunset this evening.

29th March – [Petworth.] Another beautiful spring day – though not so sunny as yesterday. We drove to Strood Farm: parked up, and set off on our walk. Made our way along the lane towards High Hoes, then on and round to Egdean – hoards of primroses and violets along the way. A most pleasant walk, with the sound of the birds chirping merrily, as if to broadcast their joy at the arrival of spring. The most intoxicating scent wafts up from the primroses and violets.

30th March – [Petworth.] The day began very cloudy – looked like the sun would never come out! But by 11 o'clock it cleared and turned to a most beautiful spring day – very warm! We drove over to Byworth and went for a lovely walk. We sat for some while on the brow of a hill, looking down into the valley, to the gentle flowing river below. Rooks, busy in their nesting colony close by, kept up their cawing. We saw one flying with a piece of brushwood in its beak; the twig was larger than the bird – it had a job to fly. Rabbits scurried about the hedgerows – blue tits, finches and sparrows chirped in all their glory, while a distant woodpecker repeatedly laughed. Bumble bees were incessantly busy – a poor lone skylark could be heard – how abundant they were when I was a lad. Saw a couple of butterflies – red admirals. The lush grass in the meadows – that fresh spring smell – nibbled short by hoards of rabbits. We made our way back along the hard road, passing the old village shop. There we paused, and got talking to an old lady [the late - Joy Gumbral] who was working in the garden – picking flowers from the borders – primroses and daffodils. The old grocery store, she told me, was 14th century – she had worked there for the past fifty years, until it had closed just a few years ago – a most interesting old lady. Her family had lived in the village for many years, and her mother, who had died only six years ago – was well into her nineties. Her father used to kill two pigs each month, and hang them on hooks outside the shop – the hooks are still there. I took a photo of her in her garden, holding her garden fork and the flowers she had just collected. Also took several photos of various parts of the village and surrounding area. Most pleasant and interesting afternoon.

31st March – [Portsmouth, Hampshire.] Went up to the top of Portsdown Hill – overlooking Langstone Harbour; Hayling Island; Bedhampton; Portsmouth and Southampton. Beautiful clear sunny day, yet out at sea a mist rolled in to as far as the coastline – strange phenomenon! This picturesque low cloud stretched in a line along the coast to as far as the eye could see, yet it came not an inch inland, where it was clear and bright – looked quite spectacular.

With regards this strange phenomenon, Sue and I, while out walking some years ago, on Bury Hill, noticed an early morning mist had gathered in the valley, where lies Amberley and Houghton. While yet, the hills above, were bathed in bright sunlight – it created a most spectacular view of the landscape; as if in some mysterious land, where a still sea swirled in and around the depths.

1st April – [Stoughton.] Most beautiful sunny morning. Went for a walk up the old lane, and into Lordington Copse – we have spent many happy hours over the years, wandering in this old wood.

Wandered on down through the wood: the charcoal burners are still there, although not working today. Came out at our favourite spot; a rough piece of ground, almost as large as a small field – a most beautiful hidden place, with an abundance of primroses; clusters of violets; periwinkles; wood anemone's, and the little white petalled wild strawberries. And today, we saw the first bluebells out in bloom this year; only a few; and these very early, in this sheltered sun trap. While strolling along the path, I noticed a piece of flint – that on closer examination, appears as if it has been worked – it resembled a scraper: first stone age implement I have found in these woods. The birds sang beautifully as we made our way back through the cool shaded track to the end of the copse. Noticed several rabbits and lots of pheasants.

The River Ems flows for the first time in two years; maybe three: the long droughts having kept the old river beds dry for that period of time.

2nd April – [Chichester.] Went to see an old friend of ours – Margaret Derby, who lives in Jubilee Road, Chichester. Whilst there, we got talking about the history of the old City, which prompted her, to tell me about a clause in her building contract, to the effect that, owing to all the premises being built on what is thought to be a 'Roman' dump – any artefacts – pottery; coins; and metal objects found in the gardens, must be handed in to the council. The city of course being Roman.[Noviamagus]

8th April – [Stoughton.] Another beautiful day. We could not get out for a walk until just after 4.0clock this afternoon. We went over to Racton Park Farm, and wandered up through the farmyard and across the fields – a lovely walk, with the sound of the rooks busy with their nesting high up in their colony, and too, the bleating of sheep and lambs – all so wonderfully peaceful. The primroses and violets about the woodlands make a lovely picture – bluebells are beginning to bloom. The bright sun, low in the sky, threw elongated shadows over the meadows – highlighting the mounds and lumps where once the ancient Racton mansion house once stood. All that remains of this old house, is a fragment of flint wall about a metre high.

10th April – [Marden.] This evening, we went over to North Marden, where we wandered off down the fields. Most beautiful evening – the quaint little church, and sheep in the fields against the darkening sky, made a most captivating picture. The evening dew enhanced the smells of country odours, making the whole walk most pleasing – the scent of grass, rotting wood, and the perfume of flowers that is always most prominent in these two periods of the day. The gold and crimson sun; and those floating mists, that will hang about low lying meadows; the caw of rooks as they make their way home in the falling light; and the evening bird song – all adding to a most peaceful scene that soothes the ruffled spirit; and refreshes the mind.

11th April – [Harting.] An early morning haze – but it soon turned out a lovely sunny day – so we made our way over to Harting, then to Goose Green. From here, we followed the tiny stream that winds through Millhanger Copse – a most beautiful woodland glade, with clusters of primroses, violets, pink campion and ladies smock. The little river leads on to Hurst Mill – long since redundant and minus its water wheel. Yet it still stands at the head of the great millpond – a sad remnant of a one time, picturesque corn-mill. The old place, I discovered some years ago, had once belonged to a maternal ancestor – William Chalcraft, who married Sarah Jane Etherington, the daughter of an auctioneer, land and estate agent of Petersfield. The miller, Chalcraft, took possession of the mill, in 1865 –. So he and his young wife probably walked, beside this ever flowing stream a good many times. While out last year, wandering through this very same spinney, Sue stepped on a nest of vicious sand wasps. She was badly stung, from head to toe, by the angry swarm. I rushed her to Petersfield hospital, where they doused her in vinegar – which eventually eased her terrible pain.

16th April – [Selborne, Hampshire.] We went to Selborne today – pulled in by the village pond at Buriton, to eat our sandwiches in the car. The ducks had about a dozen chicks – they were most comical in their antics, darting about the water, as they will. Carried on through Hawkley, then Selborne. Went for a short walk down past the church, and along by the little winding stream. Most picturesque countryside. A class of school-children, with their teachers paddled in the river, hunting for aqua-life; tadpoles and the like, I suppose! We wandered up an old lane – dotted here and there by ancient cottages – then came back into the village. Looked into the antique shop for interesting books; but this time, found nothing to suit my liking. Decided to go to Gilbert White's house for a cream tea. On the way home, coming through Oakshott, [near Hawkley, Hants.] I took several photos of the old barn at Oakshott Mill. The gardener to the house informed me, the barn was shortly to be re-clad. So that will no doubt cause it to lose its 'olde worlde' charm. We went for a short walk beside the mill stream, along the meadow where we sat quietly for a while.

20th April – [Harting.] A day of sunny periods: still rather cold in the wind. Drove over to West Harting, then went a couple of miles further on to Quebec, where we walked the upper road. From this high point, looking north, there were the most splendid views, with cows and sheep grazing in the faraway meadows. We wandered on and down to the lower road, were, on looking up, to what we had earlier looked down on, the aspect was quite wondrous – with some dwellings, perched as they were, precariously on the edge of the steep slopes. A couple of the cottages situated on the lower escarpment, still have their old wells; each with its winding mechanism, and wooden shelter intact. Sue noticed a most beautiful spotted woodpecker, it flew up from the ground, settling on a tree close by – I had no time to photograph the bird, before it flew off. An aged farm worker, who was out walking his dog, commented on how rare it was to see these birds nowadays – we talked to him for some while, about the scarcity of various species of wild birds. He pointed out that, 'thrushes; skylarks; lapwings; bats and badgers, were these days, now quiet rare: and how fortunate we were to have seen this spotted woodpecker. He was a decent old chap in his late seventies, I should think! Yet he still finds pleasure in walking the countryside.

26th April – [Stoughton.] Very wet this morning – heavy rain. This afternoon, we drove over to Stansted, where we went for a walk. The rain had cleared up, leaving the country fresh, and refreshed. Country smells were heightened by the damp morning – May blossoms, filling the air with the most beautiful scents – bluebells enhancing the intoxicating perfumes. The olde worlde smell of farmyards; the manure in the fields were too, much heightened – the birds sang lovely. We heard the first call this year, of the cuckoo. Sounded over Stansted forest.

1st May – [Stoughton.] This evening we went over to Racton Park Farm, where we walked up the lane and across the field to the woods. As we approached the woodland, the air became heavy with the most intoxicating smell of bluebells – the sun was warm – the rooks in their colony cawed in that old familiar way! We wandered in through the copse amidst a carpet of bluebells; the woodland birds sang most beautifully. Spring lambs bleated in the fields – how English it was, all so very old fashioned – sounds as old as the hills. We carried on over to Watergate House, Locksash – the old barn there, is being converted to another luxury house – we tramped up the lane, then over to the new plantation of trees, and back down the old chalk road – most peaceful walk, wonderful birdsong this evening. Took a couple of photo's while wandering about Racton Park Farm.

2nd May – [Stoughton.] This evening, we went over to the Woodmans, walked up the lane and into the woods, [Lordington Copse.] On our way back to the car, we got talking to an elderly gentleman, who lived in one of the cottages – he has resided there all his life, (he was an old countryman, in his late 70's) said he'd seen a good many changes in the countryside about the area. He recalled the old days with noticeable affection – telling of times when the hills about here were heathland, and most of the old lanes were still chalk lanes – and too, when numerous skylarks abounded and sang in the fields. The nightingale he said was a frequent visitor to the local woodlands. In that area now, he said, it is pretty well extinct. I myself, have not heard it about the Mardens, Compton or come to that anywhere south of the downs. The only place that I know of, where it still sings each year, is Balls Cross, the other side of Petworth. [What has caused the demise of this wonderful songster, remains a mystery.]

5th May – [Southbourne.] This afternoon, Sue and I went for a walk towards – Thorney and Prinsted. While walking with Sue this afternoon, we saw not too far away, a heron being chased by several rooks; an illustration of 'strength in numbers'. Rooks seem to have a well organised way of life, with uncanny ways of communicating with each other! For I have often seen small groups band up and harass birds of prey, chasing them from their territory – they certainly rule the sky's when grouped together in a flock. This has often made me wonder whether birds have some kind of 'unknown' way of communicating. For only last autumn, while wandering along a footpath over by 'Locksash', [Stoughton] I noticed a farmworker walking towards his tractor, which he had left earlier in the field. He had probably gone off to have his lunch, and was just returning to continue ploughing! There was not a bird to be seen when he restarted work – yet, before he had travelled halfway up the length of the field, there appeared a couple of seagulls, diving and squawking as they followed his plough. I paused and scanned the sky in all directions, but could see not another seagull in sight. I waited, and sure enough, within minutes, I noticed, far away, one or two, heading in the direction of the tractor; they were coming from the south. How did they know, from such a great distance, that ploughing had re-started?

For within a few minutes, more birds appeared from the same direction, and distance. A few at a time, then, after about 5 minutes, there were hundreds following the plough, gorging on the exposed worms! So, is there some form of telecommunication amongst these birds – for there was no possible way they could see over the trees, from many miles away, this 'newly exposed' source of food.

10th May – This morning, early, the sun peeped out between black looming clouds. We've had some heavy rain, or scattered showers this past week, or two – which has to be good for the trees, shrubs and lawns, and of course, the farms. Happily, everything in the countryside, looks fresh and green – sprouting with a vigour, the likes of which, we have not seen for several years now, due to the long drought this past two seasons. Hope it is not as hot as last year – for we dearly need a change in our summer weather. Very wet all day, until 3.0pm today – I then decided to go for a walk. Went round Emsworth harbour, and back along the footpath towards Prinsted. While wandering along the narrow winding path, the sound of the cuckoo reached my ear; clear and close up – it was in a tree just ahead of me – but flew off as I approached, and settled back down into heavy foliage close by. I made my way along the coastal path, with a bracing wind blowing me along – it was a spring tide; the sea was on the ebb – it foamed in anger at the force of the southerly squalls. Windsurfers tacked to catch the full force – skimming the crest of frothing waves: a man walking his dog braved the weather: I turned and headed home.

18th May – [Petworth.] Made our way over to Byworth, set off for a walk. This is a lovely old village, with quaint cottages that straggle along the length of the road for about a mile. An ancient barn, [Hallgate Farm] by the side of the road, which is always closed when we pass by, had today, its great doors open. I peered inquisitively in, to see the structure of the old beams. Its still being used as a farm building – a tired wooden ladder led up to the granary floor – rusting scales for weighing the corn stood below. Chalk and pencil marks indicated the farmers calculations, in the computing of animal food, and sacks of grain over the years. We wandered out of the village – down towards Haslingbourne, to the river – skylarks sang beautifully. As we walked across the meadows, hundreds of tiny rabbits scurried to the hedge on our approach; a woodpecker laughed in the distance – rooks in their colony close by, incessantly cawed. Made our way across to Strood Farm, where the old wall surrounding the garden of the farmhouse, has I noticed today, two brick pillars topped with stone, with iron hinges for a gate, fitted into that stonework. But, for many years now, a wall has been built between this old farm entrance. The ox-eye daisies are out in bloom, pink campion abundant – buttercup fields look beautiful, the whole countryside looks so fresh, green and lush.

23rd May – [Midhurst.] A friend of ours, a lorry driver tells me that a little while ago, a blackbird built its nest, during the period of one weekend, in his lorry – which he uses for work everyday of the week. He (a devoted animal and bird lover) had no alternative, but to take it out from where these birds had built it; 'somewhere to the rear of the cab'. The following weekend the blackbirds built another nest, in the same place as the first time – again he had to remove it. This also happened on the third week. A most uncanny 'persistence' in our natural world.

25th May – [Lurgashall.] Beautiful sunny morning – which remained so all day. Drove to Lurgashall, to – Shopp Hill Farm. Made our way to the secluded meadow, that each year is one swaying sheet of ox-eye daisies. I took a number of photo's. It is one of those rare and beautiful fields – the very image of how the countryside looked in years gone by. Noticed several pyramid orchids growing in this ancient meadow. We walked on through the woods, up along the road, and then branched off onto another footpath. This lovely old route becomes a sunken lane, with old and interesting trees each side of you – the green woodpecker; jays and magpies were about in plenty. We walked as far as Lurgashall village and back. Then we drove over to Pheasant Court farm – [Northchapel] – where we had lunch in a sun drenched opening within the woods. [Wet Wood.] It was lovely to idle here, and take in the very peace of the place – the cuckoo kept up her calling for the whole time: could have lazed here for longer. Several brimstone butterflies about; also peacocks and holly blues: and I noticed a skipper in the ox-eye daisy field. Went on to Bignor Park fête – a wonderful old fashioned event; most enjoyable. There was sheep shearing; and the making of horse shoes by the local farrier being demonstrated – and too, a brass band; bric-a-brac, for sale, and also books; flowers; cream teas and a raffle. The house and gardens, in the surrounding countryside are quite beautiful – the view looking from the back of the house, over to the downs in the distance, is lovely.

Daniel [my son, who is a qualified Shipwright] tells me that the BBC are showing this evening, a feature on 'Tenacious;' the Tall Ship he is involved with building, for the Jubilee Sailing Trust.

27th **May** – [West Dean, near Chichester.] Another hot sunny day; so we went up on the hills for a walk – over by Chilgrove – took the steep path that leads on up to Blackbush Copse – all so very silent up there. We tramped on through the cool, damp woodland, to as far as Blackbush House – [at one time, a smallpox isolation hospital] the sight of which, brought back old memories – for we had first discovered it back in the 1970's – a kind old lady [Erica Bowen] having invited us up there at the time, for tea and cakes. She was one of those rare breeds, with an insatiable passion for the arts – a wealthy eccentric, who always loved to be in the company of artists – Andy Warhol, being one of her dearest friends. Another, artist she befriended, was my cousin, Nigel Purchase, better known for his Chichester street scenes – and it was in Nigel's art gallery, where I first met this oddly bohemian lady. A couple of my own paintings were up for sale in the gallery, and it was these pictures that brought us together. "Please – come to my little house on the hill for tea," she had said. "I'll meet you both, and take you on up there." And so we went – a long and bumpy ride, through the deep rutted lanes in her old Landrover – right to the door of Blackbush House. And there inside this house – she told us the story of the place. It had apparently been, two or three hundred years ago, an isolation hospital for smallpox – and there, inside on the walls and doors, were carved the names and initials of the poor souls who had suffered this disease all those years ago. It was fascinating to see the numerous scratchings in the stone and woodwork.

1st **June** – [East Dean, near Chichester.] Strange weather today – beautiful blue sky – tiny fluffy clouds, drifting slowly about; warm sun, when shaded from the wind; the wind blew to gale force all day – very cold, for the time of year. Went over to East Dean, [near Chichester], to see Fred. Went for a walk over Court Hill, where Fred showed me the foundations of the old house where [the late] Harry Hopkins used to live. He was a builder, carpenter and undertaker. The old house had once stood 'lonely' on the hill overlooking the village; but was pulled down, I believe, in the 1960's. Part of the foundations remain, as also does the old well, which is at present covered by a couple of railway sleepers, and fenced off with deep undergrowth about it! The well, I estimated was around four to five feet in circumference. Fred told me, he had at one time, dropped a length of rope down it, and it measured forty seven feet deep. Though it was much deeper originally, but had considerable amounts of rubble thrown down it, when the dwelling was demolished. The well, according to my calculations, would have been situated inside of the house. I took several photo's of cattle grazing on the downs. Beautiful sunny evening, though still cold and windy.

19th **June** – [Southbourne.] We took a walk down to Prinsted Harbour, and around the Thorney lanes. Nice evening – the skylarks sang in the meadows, and in the distance we heard the call of the cuckoo! Rabbits about in the fields, scurrying around in playful mood, despite the years of disease these poor creatures have suffered.

22nd **June** – [Cocking.] Drove over to Cocking this morning: parked by the little stream near the church and had a sandwich in the car: king-cups nodded gently in the flowing water. While having our lunch there was a heavy thunderstorm. After the rain had eased, we went for a walk up through the village and turned off along the path towards 'Crypt Farm'. A few hundred yards along this old lane, we spotted a heron taking off from the river – graceful old bird! I took a photo of an old cart wheel, that was fixed as an ornament against the wall of the converted barn of 'Crypt Farm'. A pair of deer antlers, nailed to a sign post, pointed out the route over the downs. We turned off towards Bepton; then wandered on, until we came out onto the Bepton road. The sound of the skylark, singing for all his worth, stayed with us as we ambled along this downy path: the hedgerows blooming with bouquets of wild roses; campion; elder and hog weed: pigeons cooed and the sound of distant rooks drifted over the fields. Cornfields and yellow rape made up the landscape, beyond which, rose the awesome bulk of Cocking Down. Sue found some wild strawberries and several blue scabious. That unforgettable perfume of wild may weed scented the air, intermingled with the heavy odour of the oil seed rape. I caught sight of a partridge, scurrying out of view in a cornfield, while distant rumbles of thunder brought yet another shower. We sheltered for a while under the canopy of an overhanging hedge. Honeysuckle was in full bloom; blackberry blossoms adorned the bushes. The walk of around 5 miles, took us, at a slow meander about 3 hours; and most enjoyable it was too – felt much refreshed by the time we had finished our ramble.

28th June – [Storrington.] Drove to Storrington, where we walked around the town. Took a path leading up to Kithurst Hill, a most pleasant walk; though not many wild flowers: beautiful views looking towards Storrington. Mullein; cranesbill and nipplewort grew in patches about the hedgerows, that flanked the lane we wandered along. A church bell could be heard, repeatedly tolling, as if to summon those in earshot to some special occasion. The sound drifted over meadows and high up onto the hills, reaching my ear, in faintly audible chimes, as if from some faraway miniature village. As I listened, it was not hard to imagine the days of long ago, when the peeling of church bells always rang out specific meanings – two for a wedding, three for a death and so on; the knowledge reaching the ears of outlying and remote villagers, as fast as that of today's convenience of telephones.

29th June – Hazy sun this morn' – clouded over this afternoon, rained this evening. Went for a walk down the coast this morning – round Thorney Island. A great abundance of mallow in the fields and paths. Close by the Great Deeps, I noticed some reed-warblers flitting about – the sound of skylarks drifted across the marshes; butterflies were out in greater numbers than yesterday.

6th July – [Petworth.] Beautiful sunny morning – turned cloudy in afternoon; still very warm – the weather is stifling – close – much as if it would turn to a storm. Drove to Sutton, then on through to 'Westlands', at Fox Hill, where we had a bite to eat in the car. Went for a walk down Blackbrook Lane, towards 'Bennyfolds'. The farm, 'Westlands' has changed much of late – the old tithe barn, so I'm told, is thought to be the longest barn in Sussex! This I did not know. We turned off to the left of the lane and ambled through 'Pondtail' Woods – beautiful woodlands; fresh and green – several butterflies about: woody browns; a blue, which I believe may have been the common blue. Caught sight of a jay, its harsh cry giving its position away, as it took flight on our approach. In a cornfield, beside the woodland, we noticed a lone deer; we watched her for some while – she knew we were there, yet stood motionless! On our return along the lane, we swung off, and walked up beside a field, to the top of a hill that commands the most captivating views of the countryside about the area – 'Westlands Farm,' to the South and 'Bennyfields' to the North. An invigorating walk – most relaxing. We got talking to one of the local farm-hands, who pulled up in his landrover. We spoke of the old people we had known – the farmers – Algie Moss; George Chandler, and other well known local names. He kindly gave us some fresh honey that he had just collected. When we left him, we went on over to Balls Cross, and wandered up the lane by 'High Buildings Farm' then branched off into the woodland. Along this path, a good distance, we came to the old ruins of what at one time, was a working farm, and farm cottage; but now in ruins. There is I am told, an old well around here, but I've never found it – albeit that I have often searched the area. Perhaps it has long since been filled in. Most peaceful walk – though did not hear the nightingale, which I have in other years listened to with joy! This old and ruined farm still has, about the vicinity, some rusting farm machinery: an old corn binder; hay rakes and old seed drills; with great rusting wheels, the rims of which have decayed away, leaving just the hubs and spokes. Many wild flowers on our walk – toad flax; feverfew campian; ladies bed straw; St. John's wort; mullion; hen bane; honeysuckle and foxgloves. The toadflax in bygone days was called by the old country people 'butter and eggs'. The juice of the plant is very attractive to flies, but at the same time, very poisonous. And hence, of old, was mixed with milk, and set down where flies resort, they were said to perish at the first sip.

7th **July** – [Southbourne.] As it was such a lovely evening we took a stroll down to Prinsted, wandered along the beach – still very warm – a few birds sing this evening – the sandpipers piping their haunting call – the sun, low in the sky, glowed scarlet. A lone heron glided along the estuary, settling on his favourite fishing ground some way off; there he waited motionless. Shafts of sunlight cut suddenly through a drifting cloud, forming an almost biblical picture. A lone bait digger ambled out across the mudflats and began digging some fair way off, his silhouette showed dark against the silvery mud.

9th July – [Emsworth, Hampshire.] We went over to Emsworth Harbour late this afternoon – walked round to the furthest side. While over there, I noticed a lone bait digger, [the late Roy Dridge] far out on the mudflats [the tide was out to its furthest point] – he was wearing thigh high waders – making his way slowly along the 'hard' towards the stony beach. He carried a bucket in each hand, along with his wooden 'mud-flats,' for walking on. I photographed him as he got nearer – then, when he came up to me, I got talking to him. His name he said, was Roy Dridge – he was 76 years old, and was a 'cockler' – he went on to tell me, that he collects cockles in the summer, and winkles in the winter – or any month that has an 'R' in it, is good to collect winkles! The wooden 'mud-flats,' he used for walking over swampy ground, were called 'pattens'. He said that his father – Harry (Dior) Dridge was the last skipper of the oyster boat, the 'Echo', which lay a wreck in the harbour for many years. Oysters and scallops sold at Newhaven, around 1931: he [his father] was the first person to sell scallops in the London markets about that time. He went on to tell me, that he helped lay cables during the last war for mines! They had a narrow escape when a 'live' mine floated past their boat. Most of the deckhands, he said, who worked on the 'Echo' lived in South Street, Emsworth. When they got back to shore, they sold their catch, then went back to his fathers house, where the money was laid on the table and shared out. His grandfather who had a 'gun-punt' for shooting fowl, was loading his gun one day, when it exploded in his face, killing him instantly.

11th July – [Stoughton.] Drove to Deanlane End, and parked in the lane that leads up to South Holt Farm. The cornfields all about here, had been cut and baled up. The farm house I could see, was a lovely old place commanding beautiful views out to as far as the sea and the Isle of Wight. A deer approached from the copse across the field and wandered out; pausing occasionally to graze – then disappeared into the spinney close by. I walked along the lane that takes a course towards Forestside. This stone track was once the main highway from Portsmouth, and would almost certainly have been the route taken by those notorious smugglers, the 'Hawkhurst' gang – who took two excise men captive. They took them to 'Ladyholt Park' [1747] and there murdered the two men – Daniel Chater and William Galley. Along this lane, about half a mile, stands an old flint cottage, no longer in use. [This lovely old dwelling has long since been renovated.] It was at one time, an old keeper's cottage, and although, always, locked and shuttered up; I was, a couple of years ago, given permission by the farmer to look inside. It seems that it was last lived in over eighty years ago – and has not been touched or altered since. Everything is just how it was in those days – with old cast iron fireplaces and range in the kitchen, along with the built-in bread oven. The walls, on the inside are of wattle and daub, the exterior being flint – this of course, would have been added after its initial construction. I took a number of photographs of the old place, both inside and outside. As I wandered up the lane, the deer I had seen earlier, suddenly appeared, looked at me, then bolted off into the wood.

12th July – [Heyshott.] Drove to Heyshott Green, where we parked up and made our way towards Dunsford House, then on to see the 'Obelisk'. The stream, that glides down past Dunsford House, to join the Rother, has a special charm – weaving through old woodlands, fern covered banks and hazel copses in the most picturesque way. Honeysuckle; foxgloves and pink campion are still abundantly seen – we also noticed the yellow loosestrife. The birds are singing less now, being that time of year, when their tuneful strains become less noticeable. Butterflies are about more though! We noted the beautiful white admiral close to Heyshott. From the obelisk, we took the path that circles round and across the meadows towards Hoe Copse, then back to the car. Took the route home through Bepton – Didling to Harting. Parked up at Didling church, where we went in – most peaceful place, so quiet, inspiring thoughts of old: of shepherds long gone. I lingered by the churchyard – not a sound could be heard – no outside noise – no engines, or aeroplanes. In the hush, I caught the cawing of faraway rooks – the distant bleating of sheep – surely – a glimpse into the past. Time stood still – there was no reason to hurry – no cause to rush – a soothing moment of peace, captured in time. We wrote a few words in the 'visitors' book, signed and dated, then continued on our way home.

13th **July** – [Graffham.] Warm, but cloudy this morning – came out bright and sunny this afternoon. Drove to Graffham this morning – parked by the church, where we set off for a walk down the hill – turned off at the bottom onto the footpath leading to Tagents Farm; then cut a course across the meadows to Woodcote Farm. This farmstead, I'm heartened to note, is still a working unit – mostly dairy. We ambled on up the farm lane towards Hayland Farm. The landscape all about here, has a wonderful rolling appearance; typically Sussex. That beautiful blue bell flower, the columbine was out in bloom, along this old lane. We soon reached Haylands, a most attractive house in appearance – 16th century – a rather rambling place, with barns and outbuildings. Leaving this old place behind, we climbed halfway up the hill, to look down onto the vista below. Found an abundance of scabious growing about the hillside. Turning back towards Graffham, we took a most pleasant path: trees flanked the route: teasels dotted about here and there; and too – the white campion; a most unusual flower; also rose bay willow herb. [Old country people say, that an intoxicating drink can be made from the root of the rose bay willow herb.] On reaching the road again, down by Ladywell Cottage, a small derelict building, virtually covered in ivy, caught my attention. It was constructed of flint, with three lancet windows built into each end. The door, I noticed was of a fair age, with an old ornamented wrought iron handle. Surrounding the door on the outside, are the remains of plasterwork, upon which were daubs of colour – evidence, that at one time it had been painted, possibly with designs or pictures; it was difficult to make out. In fact, this old building turned out to be, as I suspected a long since redundant Congregational chapel – thought to have been built about 1830 – de-consecrated in 1908. Inside the chapel, is an old well, which in days gone by, supplied the whole village with their water! The chapel, may have been built over the well; the well being of much greater age – it could have been an ancient 'Holy' well. I took a couple of photos of this most interesting building.

20th **July** – [Barlavington.] Most beautiful hot and sunny day, with a pleasant breeze.

Between Duncton and Bury, nestle the beautiful old villages of Barlavington, Sutton, Bignor and West Burton: the latter being a hamlet made up of the most picturesque thatched and tiled cottages. It was in this old hamlet that this morning we wandered, with a purpose of snapping a few photos.

From West Burton, we drove to Bignor, where we set off on our walk to Barlavington, via Sutton; a more peaceful setting would be hard to find. The path leads away from the village through a sloping meadow, where glides a beautiful stream – I caught the splash of a tiny waterfall close by. Soon we found ourselves in a strip of woodland. The air was fresh – sweet smelling: the damp odour of woodland plants refreshed the spirit! Beyond the church at Sutton, the path leads over to Barlavington; the Downs dominating the landscape. We slipped down to where another stream flowed – I took a few photos of an old stone bridge; a miniature construction of considerable age. Barlavington, is one of those villages which has so few houses, that one wonders why such a spacious church was ever constructed in such a tiny, remote place. Leaving the peaceful old village, we climbed Barlavington down – an exhausting route, but well worth the effort: those breathtaking views; the downs stretching away to the east; closer to hand, the villages and their churches, where before we had walked. The sky, clear blue, with those pure-white, cotton-wool clouds, that sail lazily about on hot days! Butterflies, roved incessantly, crickets were in full chorus – we bathed in the soothing peace of the day. Surely – no greater charm than an English landscape? From here we made our way back to Sutton, to the car. We then drove on over to Midhurst – called in at Fitzhall for a cream tea: then set off from the house, on a walk through the woods. I took some photos looking from the woodlands through an old wicket gate that opened out onto a meadow. The woodland ants were about in hoards. Later, we drove over to Didling, where meadowsweet grows in abundance along the hedgerows; other flowers we found today were – broom, wild thyme, heather, and mullien: wildlife noted – a green-woodpecker; a greenfinch; a hawk and a most beautiful hare, quite the largest I have seen; we spotted too, the holly blue, comma and red admiral butterflies.

9th August – [Sutton, West Sussex.] Went over to Sutton, where I stopped to take a few photo's of the village. Got talking to an old village resident – [the late] Mr. Timlick – he was sitting quietly in his garden. He was eighty nine years old, he told me, and had worked all his life as a gardener at the Barlavington House estate – his cottage has always been tied to the job; and in his retirement, he still enjoys living there. His wife died over twenty years ago! He was a cheerful old chap. His father he said, was also a gardener; and one day, when he was little more than a child, his father asked him to sharpen the scythe; he apparently didn't do a very good job of it – so his dad picked up the hook, and hit him beside the ear with the flat edge of it. "I sharpened it aright then," he chuckled.

He spoke with great affection for his father – pointing out that the discipline of those days, did more good for people in their later life. He was a real old country character – I've often seen him, while walking through the village – sitting on his garden seat with a beer in his hand. He said the estate at Christmas time, always gave him a bottle of whisky as his Christmas box. I took a couple of photos of him in his garden.

23rd August – [Chalton, Hampshire.] Sue and I this afternoon, drove to Idsworth – we walked about the field where stands the church. – There was back in the 12th century, a tiny village in this field – the black death ultimately wiped it out. While in the area, we saw a most interesting wedding. The bridegroom and page boys, all in various old fashioned cars, arrived at the door of the church, which incidentally, lies in the middle of a field. The bride, with her father turned up 'traditionally late.' She got out of the car and proceeded to walk the long trek up to the church: she could easily have been driven there; but no, she decided instead, to walk the full length of the field path to her wedding. It all looked so wonderfully old fashioned – the very picture of a bride in bygone days. We wandered on over to were once stood the old Idsworth House. Here, close by the site of this mansion, are the remains of a cellar: it is so large that you could fit several double decker buses inside – we went down the steps to look at this incredible underground vault – now no more than a damp, gloomy hole in the ground.

1999

17th January – Very mild today; sunny periods. This morning, we are delivering 'Invitations' for the 'Photographic Exhibition' organised by the 'South East Arts.' Dropped off invites to friends and acquaintances who live in and around the Petworth and Midhurst area. As we were driving through West Stoke, we spotted four hares, they were chasing each other across a field that flanked the road. Two sprang out in front of the car – then raced over to the very centre of another meadow, and there they sat, motionless – most amusing to see these animals frolicking around.

This afternoon, we went over to Balls Cross, to deliver an invitation to Mr George Chandler, who farmed Pheasant Court Farm, near Northchapel, back in the late 1950's – he is now in his late 80's and long since retired from farming. My stepfather, Harry Pateman worked as 'farm labourer' for him during that period in time – and it was then, that I too, got to know him: I used to trudge through his farmyard on my way to school each morning. When I called on him today, he appeared to have no recollection, as to who I was – but I soon explained – he was then, delighted to see me again. He welcomed Sue and I into his house, and there we went over those long past times – the people we knew in those days: and of course, we spoke of old Harry. His face lit up, as he recalled the day that Harry, had asked for some manure to put on the garden. "By all means Harry, I'll bring a trailer load over to you straight away!" he had assured the old rustic. And so it was, that an enormous cartload of dung made its way to the old man's garden, and there it was duly dumped. Old Harry, spent the weekend spreading it over the three-quarter of an acre plot – when finished, it lay evenly over the ground to a thickness of twelve to fourteen inches; which made it impossible to dig with a spade. Of course, the old man, being a cunning sort of chap, knew only too well that this would be the case – but that was all part of his scheme. For, come Monday morning, his first words to George Chandler were, "That dungs gone on too thick for me to dig in governor – will ya come and plough it in for me?"

"Well, of course, I went and ploughed it for him!" laughed George Chandler, as he told me the story. "He weren't so silly as people made out," he concluded.

24th January – [Lodsworth] Nice weather; hazy sun – felt very much like spring – even the birds thought so, they sang quite lovely all day long. We drove over to Lodsworth this morning, as there are signs that Woolhurst Farm, will soon be converted. I intend to make a photographic record of this old place – since it is one of those very rare farmsteads that have remained untouched by the hand of the developer. The farmhouse looks of great age, as also do the several barns that are clustered around the dwelling. To see this farm, as it is today, is to look upon a scene that has remained untouched for hundreds of years – your eyes take in the very same working farmyard, that the yeoman saw two or three hundred years ago. There before you, are the old sheds, cattle hovels and the great barn, all in varying conditions of disrepair, due mainly to years of overwork, more than any purposeful negligence by the farmer. The very essence of the place is something that cannot be artificially manufactured, it comes only with age and the natural course of everyday rural industry – and once this has gone, its gone forever. [Woolhurst Farm has, since the above was written, undergone, complete renovation – it is now, no longer a working farm – and may well, never be again.]

6th February – [Stoughton.] Hazy sun, pleasant morning. We went over to Racton, and took a walk up the old stony lane to the 'Tower,' then carried on towards Stansted. Some small flint barns [New Barn Cottages,] that lay along this route, have some years ago, been converted to dwellings. The blanket of snowdrops that once grew in the Stansted woods, are no longer there ; that strip of woodland is now fenced off. A few violets and snowdrops growing along the banks of the old gravel lane. We returned along the same path. The river at the foot of the hill, is very high; the water so very clear. Here, we crossed the road, and set off up to Racton Park Farm – always a lovely walk. The rooks, busy with their nesting; constantly cawing – sounds so very old fashioned – flocks of sheep about the fields and folds close by the barns. Soon the bleating of the lambs will broadcast the arrival of Spring.

7th February – [Coldwaltham.] A most beautiful sunny morning – but a very cold wind. Set off for Coldwaltham, where I met the farmer of Waltham Farm – Mr. Roy Cooper, one of the 'old school' of farmers. A man I should think, in his seventies, full of old country stories; he told me he was hand milking the cows when he was eight years old – a splendid old chap! I took several good photo's of his farm barns – they are to be 'converted' in the near future; planning permission having been applied for. Roy Cooper spoke with great regrets at the possible closing of Guildford Cattle Markets. He felt, I believe, that which so many of our farmers and country people feel, a sad loss at all the terrible changes that are taking place these days in the countryside. Where I wonder will it all end? He remembers well, all the old farmers of Sussex who once met at the cattle markets! He knew many farmers, that I also know.

Shortly after we had arrived home, a dark black cloud appeared and it snowed hard for about ten minutes – then it cleared over, and came out bright and sunny again.

13th February – [Northchapel.] A dark damp morning. But about 9.0'clock, the sun broke through, and it turned out to be a glorious sunny day. We went to Northchapel, to Mitchel Park Farm, to photograph the old barns and the staddle barn. This done, we wandered on towards Shillinglee Lake; where there, we saw, high up in the clear blue sky, a hot air balloon – jolly cold up there I should think! But the air today, feels like spring has arrived.

20th February – [Petworth.] A beautiful mild, early spring morning. Hazy sun all day. We drove over to Westlands Farm, [Blackbrook Lane, Petworth,] wandered down through the woods, [Pondtail Copse,] a most beautiful, peaceful walk – bluebells and wild daffodils are pushing up through the mossy ground in this old spinney – they won't be long before they are all out in full bloom. Hazel catkins and primroses are out – the wonderful scent of early spring in the air.

27th February – [Itchingfield.] Went over to Possession Farm, Itchingfield, where I spoke to the old farmer who looked for all the world, like he had dropped out of the pages of a Victorian book! He was a bow legged and ancient man! He told us of a barn that belonged to his farm – that was – in the olden days, used for hanging people – they were tried by a court that was held in the old house close by, then 'hung' in the barn, he told us. We walked over the fields to see this most interesting and ancient building – it was very muddy going – but well worth getting a couple of wet feet and covered in mud to see it! I took several photo's of the old barn. Very pleased to have found this place. Mr. Scott, [the elderly farmers son,] told me of the tale that had come down in his family, regarding the old farm house, and the 'Hangman's barn! "The farmhouse," he said, "was reputed to have been used as a 'Court room' – during the 'Bloody Assizes' in 1685! When found guilty those tried, would be hung in that barn. When the Judge was in the court, he would put his coach into the cart shed close by!" which I photographed; along with the old farmhouse. This ancient dwelling has 17 rooms, and is reputed to be 900 years old.

6th March – [Ebernoe] Fine sunny morning. We drove to Balls Cross – went over to Crawfold farm, to photograph the barn. Primroses, catkins and pussy willow are all out along the lanes.

13th March – [Ebernoe.] A most beautiful sunny morning. Went to Ebernoe and parked at Colehook: walked down past the row of houses towards old Carvers cottage; which is in fact, no longer there – demolished in the 1960's. We did not wander far, as the old sunken lane was deep in mud – we had no 'wellies,' only leather walking boots. Wandered back up the way we had come, then turned off onto the track that cuts across the fields to Ebernoe. Along this well trodden route, we saw the most beautiful yellowhammer – the first I've seen for some years. We came out of the second field – where there is a most beautiful old, unaltered barn [Colhook Farm Barns] (very picturesque) and then trekked through the wild daffodil wood.

20th March – [Sutton – West Sussex.] Drove over to Sutton, then on to Glatting Farm – some wonderful old barns there, which I photographed. The farmers little dog, a Corgi, came out barking and snapping at my feet – if it wasn't for the fact that it was so vicious, it would have been funny – when considering the size of it! The owner of the house raced over to me, and apologised for his dogs behaviour – I told him I was making a record of old farm buildings – he was very interested in the project. All the lanes about here are lined with clusters of celandines and primroses – beautiful bouquets of spring flowers.

27th March – [Ebernoe.] Most beautiful sunny day. Went over to Balls Cross – walked over to Elkham Farm which I photographed. While there we strolled about the vicinity of the farm barns and picked up some beautiful pieces of pottery shards, and bits of porcelain ornaments – a tiny figure head – the torso of a person praying – they must have been exquisite pieces when complete! There were also fragments of medieval pottery about the area – all of which are the remains of the old farm house – bulldozed to the ground in the 1950's – 1960's period! Found also a piece of pottery with writing on it – 'Otway – general stores – Petworth'. This evening, I spoke to Peter Jerome, M.B.E. who told me that Otways had a general store in Petworth at the turn of the century (1900), now International Stores [Co-op]

4th April – [Tillington.] Walked from the top of River, down 'Janes Lane;' – a deep sunken lane, with natural rock formations, above which, a canopy of broad leafed trees, acts as a cool shade on hot summer days. At the top end of this path, there is an old farmhouse, with stone mullioned windows, and a high garden wall, made up of sandstone blocks. Now, these great stone blocks, appear too well cut for a simple garden surround; – they, in fact, look so odd in their position, that I have often wondered whether they are salvaged from the ruins of the 'lost' Chapel of River – the site of which, is situated, in the middle of the field, which lies South, West of 'River Park Farm'. A most beautiful old fashioned walk; the lane is full of primroses; violets and snowdrops, and in the woods are wild daffodils. We wandered past Roundabouts Farm, then on up Westlands Copse lane to Kimbers Cottage. The birds sang wonderfully. Most lovely day.

10th April – [Harting.] Went over to Turkey Island: walked along lanes and over fields – very peaceful. Many lambs – how delightful to hear their constant bleating – see their boisterous frolics – leaping and running about the fields – we spent some time watching them. This old village, had at one time, an ancient chapel – the sight of which has long since been lost. Walked on over to West Harting – to Pays Farm, which has recently been sold – the barns up for conversion. The farmer was working in the farmyard, so I asked him if I could photograph the barns before they were altered; he was quiet happy for me to do so. There were several farm-trailers, and miscellaneous bits of machinery blocking the view of the great barn – but I took several pictures of the other farm buildings.

16th April – [Birdham] Heavy frost again last night – hence, bright and sunny morning. Drove over to Itchenor – took photos of Holt Place Farm – the old flint barns, with clock tower built aloft. This building, I am reliably informed, was used in the 'First World War,' to house the fire-engines, that put out the fires during the German bombing raids in the area.

17th April – [Wiston.] Bright sunny morning – thicker clouds later, though still bright at times, with odd shower about. Went over to Wiston, and walked down the old rutted lane which passes through the Great Barn Farm: took photos of the farm buildings, then ambled on towards the Manor House. A wonderfully old fashioned walk – primroses and bluebells out in all their glory. On our way back up the lane, we met a friendly tractor driver who works on the farm – we chatted a while about farming; and how he missed the old ways of working the land.

18th April – [Woodmancote, near Hurstpierpoint.] Frost again last night – fine sunny morning. The village of Blackstone still retains an untouched, old world charm. There are here a couple of old farms that are still working, and the old cottages appear as they have always looked. The air, as you walk down the little street, is heavy with the old fashioned smell of busy farmyards – giving the place a unique appeal.

24th April – [Petworth.] This afternoon, we drove over to Rotherbridge and took a walk down past Kilsham Farm. Lovely old lane, full of wild flowers; the sweet scent of bluebells, violets and primroses all adding to the country perfumes that hang in the air. Rotherbridge Farm, was much altered – all the barns are now 'converted:' – a radio blared out a deafening noise as we went by, polluting the very peace of this country lane. Birdsong was drowned out by a torrent of 'heavy metal.' We hastened a retreat back to the car, and made our way over to Fox Hill – Blackbrook Lane, and there took a walk down through Pondtail Copse – a most beautiful patch of woodland. Was that the nightingale I heard? – I could not be certain – too early, surely! Gentle breezes occasionally fanned the scent of the bluebells – this sweet intoxicating air wafting up and mixing with the other woodland smells. Clusters of violets still growing along the banks of Westlands lane.

25th April – [Compton.] Went to Up Marden – looked around the little church: very peaceful place – remnants of wall paintings – discovered under the layers of whitewash! These old paintings I suppose, were covered over by the painters during the Cromwellian war. We walked across the field from the church – then out onto the road and into Binkard Copse. Quite beautiful with the whole woodland a carpet of bluebells. Wandered across the field and onto the path that heads down to 'Wildham Barn.' [now sadly converted] Lovely old walk along here. Returned along the lane by Up Marden Church. Peered into the old open cart-shed – marvellous construction. Though now fallen into ruin – with ivy and brambles almost covering it. Inside, leaning up against an oak beam, are a pair of wagon shafts – no doubt, deemed redundant years ago – the old cart, having long since rotted away. Also in this barn, are an archaic set of wooden harrows, complete with the towing brackets that hitched onto the harness of the great heavy horses of the olden days. It must surely be a museum piece! Another barn close by houses a redundant 'elevator': once used on the farm for lifting bails of hay or corn up onto ricks.

2nd May – [Southbourne.] Start of Millennium photo shoot – the first being – the Rev. Clive Jenkins and the congregation of St. John's Church, Southbourne, near Chichester. It took some time to bustle the crowd together for a good picture – but it came right in the end – and so, with many smiling faces the first Millennium photo was done.

[The above event, was the first of a number of 'photo-shoots' – designed to mark the Millennium 2000, with a series of pictures depicting groups of villagers, gathered together in their respective village. All the photographs, consequently appeared in the 'West Sussex Gazette'.]

[Fittleworth.] This afternoon we drove over to Fittleworth, where a number of the villagers had opened their gardens to the public. The first we visited was 'The Grange' – a magnificent old house beside the river, with the garden reaching down to the water. They had cultivated a piece of ground to make a 'thyme' lawn, an ancient way of making a perfumed lawn! Our next garden was at 'Hesworth Grange', built around 1790. We had a most enjoyable walk up the old lane to this house. Very peaceful place, with a garden, old in style, falling away from the house to meet the boundary hedges, where beyond lay old fashioned meadows, untouched by the plough. Our next house was 'Birch Walk House, which has a wild garden – steep in places; covered in a blanket of bluebells. Glorious shrubs – rhododendrons, made a lovely picture. Our next house was 'Fittleworth House', a most interesting place with a Georgian front: but some parts were undoubtedly, much older. The largest cedar tree I have ever seen, grows in the garden; the girth, close to the ground, was I believe, at least eight feet in width, A holly tree had taken root in the crux of one of the bows of this magnificent tree, and was growing quite happily. In the garden was a stone seat, with an embossed Tudor Rose emblem; it looked of great age. The main gate, was bricked up between two old pillars. 'Manville Field' house had a very pleasant garden; the house though was modern. 'Hampton Cottage' was very interesting: it was a quaint little dwelling, with a beautiful old fashioned cottage garden. The owner had collected many bygone artefacts – shop signs, and numerous other, long since redundant relics, which he had found over the years. He had made a quaint little grotto in the garden, in which was a 1930's radio, a gramophone, magazines, and books all of that period. Music was playing in this little retreat, the melodies giving an atmosphere of having slipped back in time. Our next place was 'Devon House' another quaint cottage and garden, with a little burbling stream running down through it! Our next house was 'Le Ruissoau' a most intriguing place – the area on which it was built, was at one time a quarry – two old army huts, which had been brought by the owner many years ago, had been put there: he had spent the ensuing years building a most interesting construction – with wooden balconies and all kinds of strange ideas. Our last house was 'Chapel

Bank' a modern house, with breathtaking views looking over to the distant downs. Was this, I wondered, the site of some long lost chapel?

3rd May – [Petworth.] Another beautiful warm, sunny day. We drove over to Selscome Farm, to see David Burden, (farmer) as I had arranged to take some photographs of his flock of sheep. Met his family – took a few pictures around the farmstead – then set off in his daughter Helen's car. Made our way over to farmland that is all part of Burton Park House. I snapped photos of his sheep as we wandered around the fields; then we drove on over to Cooks Farm, at West Burton – took more photos of yet another flock – also some of the huge barn, which is of a great age. Made our way back to David Burden's place – had a cup of tea, then came away. He was well pleased with the 'photo shoot.' It was gone two, by the time we left the farm. We drove to Balls Cross, and went for a walk through the bluebell woods, [Bittles Field Copse] where we have often heard the nightingale – but did not hear its fluting notes today. Wandered down through the woodlands and out onto the old meadow – where there were hundreds of early purple orchids in full bloom.

10th May – [Fishbourne / Appledram.] Sunny periods – quite windy. We went over to Fishbourne creek; blowy beside the water. The meadows still look as they did over forty years ago – unploughed, strewn with buttercups: the air still has that enduring smell of salt, tinged with a whiff of celery – which it had when I was a boy. The reeds still grow in profusion, and ducks still rear their chicks on the pond – nice to see it alters but little. From here, we walked to Dell Quay: a number of changes over the past half century, have taken place though, along this part of the inland waterway. As a boy [in the early 1950's] I used to wander over the 'Westgate fields,' from Chichester, to this pretty harbour. There was, in those days, an old converted naval barge, moored halfway between Fishbourne and dell Quay – it was known locally as the "Tea-boat." And it was here, that families came of a weekend, to have tea and cakes in the upper cabins; and while doing so, enjoy peeping through the portholes, at the wonderful sea-views. This old boat is now no more – a few oak beams left in the mud, mark the spot where once it lay. Further along the coastal path, towards the quay, there was also, a row of houseboats, one beside the other – each one lived in by old fishermen and their families.

They too, have now all gone. Hawthorn and blackberry bushes, used to grow alongside the water – edging the path and fields – some shrubbery still remains; though not so prolific. Not too far from the quay, on the hard, near the pub, a redundant naval boat lay for many years. This old wartime gunboat, was painted with 'red-oxide', and was consequently, always known as the 'Redboat'. We would play around on this old vessel – climbing down into the cabins and about the decks. Its now long since gone – brought and converted to a houseboat, I believe. We often walked along the reedy shore to Birdham – sometimes we would paddle out at low tide to the far side of the harbour. [Bosham] One day we did that and the tide came in – we had to wave to someone on the far side of the estuary, who had a small rowing boat – they came over and pulled us out of the mud. And did we get a telling off from the old fisherman. All those old memories came flooding back to me today.

15th May – [West Dean.] Lovely sunny morning – but looks like its threatening rain – with dark clouds looming in fast from the north. Drove to West Dean – parked by the pub and walked up along the road a little way, then made a detour off, and onto the old disused railway – went under the bridge and along the line – a most beautiful hidden track. The broad leafed trees and hedgerow bushes, form a glorious shaded walk: plush green mosses and ferns grow along this damp secluded route. We trekked on for some good distance, before deciding to turn back to the road – I had hoped to photograph a barn that lies out across a field, but it was on private land, so was impossible to get to without further permission. Back to the car – and we drove on over to Didling – parked by the tiny old shepherds church, and made our way up the steep sunken lane that leads to the top of the hill. The birds were in full song – their voices floating through the trees in unison – all species singing together. Lapwings dived about the fields below us, sporadically crying in alarm at the marauding rooks: lambs played in the grass – it was a glorious moment caught in time – nature at its most beautiful – the sun even burst out of the clouds for a while, as if to add to the splendour of the moment.

29th May – [Northchapel.] Went over to Upper Frithfold Farm, and from here we set off on our walk. Heard the nightingale singing, as we made our way up the lane. At the farm they were busy sheep-shearing; and as we passed by, one of the shearers bawled out, "good-day to ya!" in a broad Australian voice. We replied with a friendly wave of the hand, then wandered on through fields of shorn sheep – soon reaching Roundwhyke House. Close by this great rambling farmhouse, there stands a lovely little cottage; derelict, and falling to ruin. [This tiny dwelling has since been renovated, and is now occupied.] The old meadows about here looked lovely – full of buttercups, that nodded in the warm, gentle breeze. The footpath appeared little used, overgrown with weeds and long grass, which made the going difficult.

31st May – [Steyning.] Went to Steyning, to the Whitsun Country Fair. Every year, when this event is on, they close the road which runs through the town. The stallholders, pitched along the high street, were all dressed in 'old fashioned' clothes – mostly Victorian costumes, that harmonised perfectly with the old buildings of this country town. There was too, an interesting selection of farm animals, all held in their relative pens around the market square – pigs; sheep and lambs, goats, heavy horses and different breeds of fowl. An old 'threshing machine' and a 'Field Marshall' tractor drew great attention, as too did an old farmer, who had brought along a trailer loaded with redundant farm implements. The children did well with their maypole dance, all dressed in 'olde worlde' attire. The local butcher, with barbecue pitched in the high street, did an endless trade, selling hot dogs and beef burgers – the smell drifting down the street and enticing the crowds to make a bee-line for his stall. The jugglers, clowns, and local bands, kept the hoards merrily amused all day long. We left after a most enjoyable day feeling happy – but very tired.

6th June – [Fernhurst.] The weather, early this morning, was very dull – but brightened up to a nice day. Fernhurst millennium photo-shoot – the press were there, they asked me several questions about the project. After the 11.am morning service had finished, the Reverend Roake, came out to meet us and helped organise the crowd. The photo shoot went off very well.

20th June – [Bignor.] The wind blew hard in the night – driving rain hard against the windows. The Bignor millennium photo-shoot at 2.pm today – will the weather clear over? I wondered. 'Rain before seven, leave off before eleven,' is the old saying. And how true it was today – for the sun peeped out around 11.30am – it struggled furiously with the cloud cover, then finally won the day! We packed up the photo equipment and drove off to Bignor – arrived there by 1.30pm – the people were all most friendly, a really nice crowd. Took the photo about 2.15pm – then we all stood about chatting with cool drinks and biscuits – everyone was well pleased with the way it all went. "It gave them," they all said, "a good opportunity to meet and chat to their own neighbours," which from what I can make out, does not happen very often. Many said they wanted prints of this special occasion. The event was organised by the churchwarden, Mr. Nicholas Symes.

3rd **July** – [Chichester.] As arranged, we drove to Dell Quay, to meet my old friend Fred and his wife, Julie. We all wandered along the path beside the estuary, heading towards Fishbourne: it was a lovely warm evening. Fred wanted to look around a tiny pond that lies nearby in a field. We climbed the fence and ambled over to it – a filthy, oily puddle of water, with little or no wildlife in it: though I did notice a couple of moorhens paddling about. The evening was quite – very still – and in that stillness the distinct burr of the corncrake reached my ear, sounding from far across the meadows. I was surprised to hear it, since I had long believed this bird to be extinct in this part of the country – but there is no doubt, it was certainly the corncrake that we had heard.

4th **July** – [Fittleworth.] Very poor, overcast weather. Coates millennium photo-shoot today, at 11.o'clock. We arrived about half an hour early for the photo session. It being Sunday, the church service was still going on – we waited outside. And in our idleness, we wandered about the churchyard, reading the epitaphs on the headstones. It was strangely moving – to step from grave to grave, reading the names of long gone villagers, while listening to the present parishioners singing in the church; the music drifting over the churchyard, and sounding for all the world as it would have done to any of those now laying at rest – as if old England still sang on, as it had in those bygone days. The church service over, the vicar appeared, followed by the churchwarden – Mr. Wilson. After a short discussion, it was decided that, due to the poor weather, we should postpone the photo shoot until a later date – fixed for the fifth of September.

This afternoon, I had the Wisborough Green, millennium photo-shoot. The villagers had gathered outside the church – the majority of which, desired the photo-shoot to go ahead, in spite of the adverse weather. So I took the photographs – and it all went off very well – they seemed pleased with the whole occasion.

10th July – Around 5.00 pm. Colin Dunn, the editor of the 'Downs Country' magazine' came to my house, as arranged. We talked for some long while about my reasons for making such a precise photographic record of the barns and farm buildings: the subject being considered as an article for inclusion within that magazine.

11th July – [Treyford & Kirdford.] Millennium photo-shoot. Most beautiful sunny day and very warm. Went to Treyford, where I had arranged to photograph the villagers, in the garden of the Manor House, which is owned by Daniel Hodson. He and his wife and daughter, were there to meet us, with drinks – a most hospitable family. Not that many people live in Treyford, as it is only a small village. After around 3 quarters of an hour, I took the photo with the medieval dovecote as a backdrop. The villagers were very pleased with their photo and all went off very well. Continued on to Kirdford – where the Millennium photo-shoot has been arranged for 2pm today – quite a few turned up there. The organiser Ian Campbell was a decent sort.

24th July – [Clapham.] Most beautiful sunny day – very warm – hot. This morning I phoned Mrs. Eileen Cornford, of Clapham Farm, Clapham, Sussex, to see if it was convenient for us to go down to look round her farm. Mrs. Cornford, who had heard about my search for old farm buildings, had phoned me some few weeks ago, to tell me of her and her brothers – David and Peter's farm. We drove down there, arrived around 11am. Most friendly and hospitable family. David Cornford showed us around the old farm – some lovely old buildings. A tithe barn, and a brick and flint barn with its roof missing – the date of (1766) was written in the brickwork. Another interesting old construction, was a medieval dove cote – the walls of which were made of flint and malm stone, built to a thickness of four feet – the great old oak beams were rotten with woodworm. Inside, it was very cool away from the summer heat. There was also a long, squat 'redbrick' cowshed, with a tiled roof, and an impressive tall chimney, ornately designed – in a style similar to that which adorned the old farmhouse close by. The chimney breast came down into the structure, and then petered out to nothing, as if a fireplace had been taken out, and the void then blocked in. David Cornford, told me that it had never been used, and that it was in fact a 'genuine' folly.

David told me that his father – Boaz Cornford, born 1908 – died 1986 – was one of the old 'die-hard' farmers, who never changed his way of farming from the old ways – he always used an old binder and a thrashing machine – he stooked his corn, and turned the hay, in the old farming way. He even sowed his corn with an old corn fiddle – right up to his death in 1986. A most interesting family. Eileen Cornford, who was in a wheelchair, told me she had worked on the farm until she was nineteen years old, in 1950 – she had then caught 'polio,' which left her disabled. She has since done pretty well all the 'paperwork' for the smooth running of the farm – a most admirable lady – full of strong character and unending resilience. I took photographs all around the farm, and of David Cornford, holding his fathers old corn riddle.

7th **August** – [Rogate.] Sunny periods all day. Went over to Rogate to undertake the millennium photo shoot, at the village fête today. On arriving there, we met the fête organiser – Patrick La'pla, who said he would muster the people for us over the tannoy at 2.20pm. He had kindly put the event in the village fête programme. While waiting, we met Louise Adams, press reporter of the 'Chichester Observer' – she was familiar with my photo project. The time arrived for the photo-shoot – it was slow for people to gather after the announcement, but a reasonable amount turned up – including a couple of 'Lords' of the area. While taking the photo, a press photographer from the 'Petersfield Herald' took a picture of me photographing the villagers. So all went well today.

8th **August** – [Elsted.] Raining hard this morning – in fact – torrential rain! This afternoon, the weather cheered up, so we drove to Elsted, where I have to photograph the villagers on the twenty-second of this month. I wanted to look over the location – which is outside of the village hall. Captivating views from this vantage point – ideal as a backdrop for the picture. We walked down the road, in the direction of the downs – most pleasant as the sun peeped out – very warm. The trees dripped incessantly from the morning rain – everything smelt fresh and pleasant; it felt as if the earth had quenched its thirst. The sunlight sparkled on the leaves – all the countryside looked glorious. We wandered back to the village, then over to the church, and down the cool sunken lane – how many hundreds of hobnailed boots have trudged down this old path over the centuries? I wondered.

11th August – [Chichester.] A 'complete' eclipse of the sun forecast for today. But, on this hot and sunny day, we had to go to Chichester! The old city was, as usual, bustling with summer visitors. About ten past eleven, the eclipse began: some amongst the crowd paused in expectation. Then, at a quarter past the hour, it began to get darker – hundreds of people then stopped to look through their 'special' glasses, which they had brought for the occasion. By eighteen minutes past eleven, the sun was almost gone! Darkness fell over the city – there was an uncanny silence – everyone stood in awe – all peering up at the eclipse. The light was strangely eerie – an orange glow – almost dusk-like! The cathedral spire, completely shrouded in this awesome light, loomed up high in the heavens. The whole experience was most moving – it gave you at the time, the feeling that something special; something rare and exceedingly powerful was occurring – a natural force happening within our universe – that which no man could control. Even the seagulls, that are usually squawking above the streets, went silent. The hush lingered for some moments – then, it was all over – the sun returned.

It was certainly, the strangest thing I've ever seen: to be walking about the town, with the warm sun shining from a clear blue sky prior to the 'eclipse' – as was the case in Chichester. Then, within a few seconds – to see an inky shade fall over the town – the neon shop lights switched full on, as if it were the close of a dark autumn day – and too, to feel the temperature drop noticeably colder – a disturbing chill, almost like a winters evening, the effect adding to the eerie feeling of the whole spectacular phenomenon.

The Television news said later – that many thousands of people had travelled down to Cornwall – having been informed that it would be better to see the 'eclipse' in that region. But sadly, the sun never appeared in that far western county – cloud cover remained all day – while in Sussex, it was never better.

15th August – [Lurgashall.] The Lurgashall, villagers millennium photo-shoot, arranged for 11. o'clock today – I arrived about 10.20 am. David Martin-Jenkins helped to organise a lorry load of chairs – about sixty – for the elderly people of the village to sit on, in the front row. Around a hundred and sixty people are expected to turn up for the event. The sun peeped out – and those smiling band of villagers were caught on camera. Afterwards, I was asked if I would photograph an elderly lady who was unable to get to the event – "Yes, of course – I'd be most pleased to take her picture," I said. The whole photo shoot went very well.

21st August – [West Grinstead & West Hoathley.] A beautiful clear blue sky today – ideal weather for photography. Made our way over to Home Farm, Partridge Green. The farmer, [Mr Kempley] who kindly gave me permission to photograph his barn was very helpful. He thought the barn was built around 1600 – 1620. He told me, he planned to convert the building at some time in the future, as it was no longer in use. An old oak cart-shed, attached, and built at a right angle to this great 'Sussex' barn, he hoped to move piece by piece to his house and use it as a garage. The 'oak barn' which is situated in the 'working farmyard' he said, would also, have to be moved before conversion was possible – there being no proper access road to the building. He said he would dismantle the complete construction, and then rebuild it in a better position on the farm. This task he estimated, would cost around £5,000 to complete.

This afternoon, we went over to West Hoathley, looked around the most interesting churchyard. A fascinating collection of church monuments are to be seen here. The views from this churchyard are breathtaking – from the vantage point, you can see over the valley of the river

Ouse towards Lewes and the distant south downs. Near the top of the churchyard terraces, a stone bears the epitaph:-

"Friend looking out on this wide Sussex view,
know they who rest here looked and loved too,
Pray then like them to sleep, life's labours past,
In your remembered fields of home at last."

In the little 'pamphlet' we brought from the church, there is a rather amusing epitaph – taken from the grave-digger of Kingsbridge, Devon 1795. It is in reference to the 'privilege' that important members of the community have, in being buried 'within the church'. It reads:-

"Here lie I at the chapel door,
Here lie I because I'm poor,
The further in the more you pay,
Here lie I as warm as they."

22nd August – [Elsted.] The Elsted villagers millennium photo-shoot today. Fine beautiful, sunny morning – but by 10.30 am the sun begins to disappear – clouds looming. At 11.30am, we arrived, as arranged, outside the village hall. I met there Terence Allen, who was helping me organise the event – he was fairly sure all was going to schedule. Soon the villagers appeared and grouped together for their millennium photograph – it was a good turnout – everyone was well pleased.

26th August – [Treyford.] This afternoon we went over to Treyford, where we wandered over the fields: walked round the old deserted churchyard, that now has no church – spotted a squirrel. The hills looked as beautiful as ever. We wandered on up the lane to the very top, to Buriton Farm – a tiring yet enjoyable climb.

28th August – [Rudgewick.] Went over to Rudgewick steam rally, a good many exhibitors there, covering several fields. Much farming activity in the old fashioned way going on – ploughing with heavy horses; old tractors – binding corn and thrashing. We met Neil and Paula Redrove, of Ewehurst, Dorking, Neil was in charge of the threshing machine. They still thrash corn for a farmer, Verna Bailey of Billingshurst. Very interesting day.

29ᵗʰ August – [Heyshott.] Beautiful sunny morning – clouded up to a hazy afternoon. At 11am, we had the Heyshott Millennium photo shoot. All went very well – we met there several interesting people. It was an unusual event, with the inclusion of several pets – two or three dogs, and the resident pony – a most curious picture.

30ᵗʰ August – [Wisborough Green.] Cloudy morning – until midday – beautiful afternoon. Went over to Lowfold, where we had a picnic at the end of the lane. After our sandwiches, we walked up towards Steve Osmaston's farm, [Lowfold Farm.] He does not work the dairy-farm nowadays – so all was quite around the farmyard – almost eerie. I remember it as always being so very busy – full of rural industry; a humdrum of country sounds. It was a strange feeling, to stroll around the farmyard amid such silence – almost sad! A great loss – as if it were the passing of an old friend; now gone – gone forever! What shame our country; to allow 'farming' to fall into such a state. Later this afternoon we went over to the Wisborough Green fête, and spent the rest of the afternoon there. We then walked from the fête towards Haresfold Farm, I took several photos of the barns, that are scattered about the farmyard. Very enjoyable day – occasionally thought provoking.

4ᵗʰ September – [Clapham & Patching] A most beautiful sunny day. Set off about 2.15pm for Clapham and Patching, where I am to photograph at 4. pm, the villagers at their village flower show – my first – 'joint' – millennium photo-shoot. It was mid afternoon when we arrived – and the festival was in full swing. They had a couple of marquee's, one for flowers and vegetables, the other for tea and cakes: a brass band, and numerous games for the children. There was a good turnout of people from both villages. We met Pat Cleary who was organising the 'photo shoot' for me, and Sir Richard Best who was the commentator. Sir Richard, gave the photo event a marvellous boost, with plenty of encouragement. We had everyone that was at the show grouped together for the photo. All went off extremely well. Lord Somerset, was also there. We met our friends, David, Peter and Eileen Cornford, [farmers of Clapham Manor Farm] at the event. They were pleased to see us – we promised to go and visit them again very soon. We stayed until the end of the annual village event.

5th September – [Fittleworth.] Most beautiful sunny day. Coates village millennium photo-shoot today at 11am. Met Vivian and Terri Miles at the church, they are both helping to organise the event. Most of this tiny scattered community turned up for the photo and all went well. Vivian and Terrie Miles asked us back to their house for a coffee; we walked over there, as it's only a few minutes from the church. In bygone days, their dwelling was I believe, the old gate-house to the castle. Gathered in their lounge – we sipped hot drinks, and chatted about the villagers millennium photo project, and how important it will be as a future historical document. Steven Guy who lives at Coates Castle, asked if I would, sometime in the future, photograph the residents of the castle – he led us over to the old picturesque building, so that I could see the best place to photograph the residents. In the grounds of the castle, there is a chestnut tree, of an enormous circumference – it must have been planted at the same time as the castle was built, I should think.

11th September – [Heyshott.] We went over to Heyshott, where there was an 'Old Fashioned Farming' event on there this weekend. Spent the afternoon there – walking around and photographing the motley assortment of rural people that were demonstrating, or exhibiting their country crafts at the show. Mr. J.A. Reed of Shere, Guildford, was demonstrating the making of ropes, and how you make linen from flax. Photographed Mike Bridger, ploughing with an old tractor and Clive Kennett, who was ploughing with two shire horses named Brigadier and Clyde. From the show-ground we walked up a lovely old chalk lane towards the downs – and looked back down on the agricultural show – how English it all looked – a mist formed in the distance – serenely quiet – beautiful scenery.

12th September – [Compton, West Sussex.] Weather – much cooler today – long cloudy periods, with glimpses of sun. Villagers Millennium Photo-shoot today – Compton, near Chichester. Mr. Lemon of that village helped me organise the event. A good many people turned up, despite the small size of the village. The only place suitable to take the photograph was in the farmers, somewhat overgrown meadow. The project went off very well – everyone seemed to enjoy the it. Though, shortly after I'd taken the picture, one little lad, of perhaps six or seven, years old, fell into a patch of stinging nettles – he cried much, poor little chap! His parents rubbed him down with dock leaves!

19th September – [Elsted, Treyford, Kirdford and Coates] Very wet all day – most miserable. This afternoon, we delivered some of the Millennium photographs. First to Elsted, where Terence Allen asked us in for a drink – while he examined the photo. We chatted for around an hour, he was well pleased with the picture. Daniel Hodson of the Manor House, Treyford asked us in, he was also pleased with the photograph, as too was Ian Campbell of Kirdford, and Viv Miles of Coates.

26th September – [Stoughton & South Stoke.] Most beautiful day for village millennium photo shoot. Arrived at Stoughton at 11am for 11.15 photo shoot. An average number of people arrived for so small a village! Met Mrs. Langmead – she asked if it was possible for me to photograph, at a later date, owing to a number of people who were unable to get to this event – her husband and their farm workers! Regrettably it was not possible to make another date for this year – but I suggested, we organise a date next year. Photo shoot went off well, in spite of it being difficult for me to find a suitable position to take the photograph.

This afternoon, we drove over to South Stoke, where we had a picnic. We then looked around the lovely old church – all decked out with vegetables and sheaves of corn for the 'harvest festival' – to start at 3pm. As we were coming away, the congregation were arriving! The old house, [at one time, the village Inn] which stands beside the little wicket gate, as you enter the churchyard, displays on its wall, a great confusion of graffiti – probably, the initials of village sweethearts of long ago. In the church yard, we noticed a gravestone – Alfred Bond, aged 19years – drowned in the river Arun – late last century. A most dangerous river – many people drowned in it over the years. We walked down to the river – water very high today – what with the excessive rain of late, along with the high tide. Ambled along the tow path towards Arundel – many giant dragonflies – counted eight in all, flying together in one particular place. Took a few photo's of the tiny village from the fields, with too, a strangely picturesque dead tree in the fore ground. The sky was black with storm clouds, while the bright sun highlighted the whole enchanting picture. A most pleasant walk.

2ⁿᵈ October – [Northchapel.] Sunny periods – nice photography weather. Went over to Northchapel in afternoon. Went for a walk down the old lane towards Middle Diddlesfold. Wandered over the ploughed fields, where across the way, we picked up several pieces of medieval pottery. Sue spotted an old black glass button, possibly Georgian – she also found an interesting stone – one side of it being worn down flat. Was it. I wondered, an old cobble-stone? Or was it a stone for sharpening scythes – what the rustics of Sussex, used to call a 'pommy-stone'?

3ʳᵈ October – [Nuthurst.] Cold wind – though beautiful sunny day. Millennium village photo shoot today – Nuthurst. After the church service – it being Sunday – we met Mrs. Denise Middleton, who was organising the event. About fifty people turned up for the photo – all went off very well. Very picturesque Victorian church, both inside and outside! We went round to the village hall after the 'photo session' for a coffee.

10ᵗʰ October – Dull, dreary weather – all day. Drove to Treyford, as previously arranged, in order to photograph Mrs Napier, the churchwarden – she having missed the village millennium photo-shoot: took several pictures of her in the garden. She then asked us in for a cup of tea – we chatted about the event, and the church – she tells me, she sings and plays the organ there each Sunday. Our mission complete, we came away and drove over to Balls Cross. Ambled up the old lane to Crawfold Farm – then on through Crawfold Copse, where, just across the fields lies Medhone Farm – once the site of an ancient chapel – it stood there, apparently, up until the early seventeenth century. A most peaceful walk – the woodlands having that damp autumn smell – the odour of rotting vegetation, mixed with high scented fungus – numerous fungi about the woods.

17ᵗʰ October – [Petworth.] Drove to Fox Hill: turned off down Blackbrook Lane, and parked up near Westlands Farm – made our way down the lane, then turned into Pondtail Copse: clusters of fly agaric fungi have sprung up in this damp woodland. We sauntered on towards Moor Farm – Several people fishing in the great ponds – spotted a most beautiful kingfisher darting across the lake – a spectacular blue, green sheen. A relaxing walk on this wonderfully pleasant autumn day.

24th October – [Emsworth, Hants.] Around midday, we went to Emsworth. Spring tides are very high – made worse by the gale-force winds and heavy rain. Roads flooded in this small town – the local sailors have great concern for their boats in the harbour. Water has flooded over the barrier wall, which holds back the sea from the millpond. Winds and rain eased a little by late afternoon – though the sky still looks full of it!

6th November – [Selsey & Sidlesham.] Went to photograph the great flint barn, belonging to Coles Farm – the farm buildings are in ruins – falling down through neglect – due to lack of use. The 'church', so I am told, are the owners of the property? From here we went on over to Pigeonhouse Farm, Church Norton, where there are some interesting farm buildings. The farm at one time was part of the ancient priory. I happened to meet, on enquiring for permission to photograph the place, a friendly farmhand, who apparently lived in the old granary. He most kindly, showed me around the farmstead. The 'medieval' pigeon-house, [hence the name of the farm] with its original, purpose built pigeon-holes, I noticed, still remained intact – the other outbuildings I found, equally as interesting. The farmhand who acted as my guide, was a most unusual person too. For he had the appearance of having slipped out of the pages of a Thomas Hardy novel – a wild looking character, with a great bushy beard – yet with a jovial face, and a most friendly nature.

This afternoon, we went over to Sidlesham, where I met the farmer of Kipson House Farm, with a view to photographing his farm buildings. He was most helpful – we chatted a great deal – said, he was like most farmers these days, feeling the 'squeeze' of the times. He went on to tell me that, when he was a young man back in the fifties, this farm was a most picturesque place, with all the old farm buildings unaltered. He said there was a most beautiful thatched oak barn there too, which he had, some good many years ago, pulled to the ground – "Worst days work I ever done!" he grumbled with a note of sadness. "It was" he pointed out, "a most beautiful building – a great thatched tithe barn – now gone forever!" I photographed some of the old buildings that still exist.

7th **November** – [Harting.] Went over to East Harting, where we had a picnic, then we took a most enjoyable walk. The air was sweet and clear, very autumnal – trees turning to a wonderful bronze. Countryside looks so colourful. Met a retired farmer feeding the ducks in the village pond. A very friendly old chap – he feeds them every day, at the same time. They looked so funny as they all trooped in single file up the road towards him – hastening after their grain.

19th **December** – Snowed hard during the night – snow drifts this morning: very cold – still freezing! Took some time to clear the car windscreen – shortly after 10.o'clock, we set gingerly off – heading for Upwaltham – got no further than St Mary's farm – here, the police had blocked off the road, "it being too dangerous," they said, the only way to get to Upwaltham, was to drive round East Dean – which we did. The countryside along this lovely old byway was quite beautiful – a clear blue sky, with the sun shining brightly onto snow covered trees – a perfect winter wonderland. We parked up at Upwaltham, and made our way over to the farm – took several photos, then trudged up the hill towards Shepherds Copse. I snapped a few more pictures from this high point, looking, as we were, down towards the church – took some of Sue, wrapped in her scarlet coat – how she stood out amidst the pure white background – quite stunning. The drifts were deep and picturesque.

2000

1st January – At midnight, on this first day of the year – the resounding sound of fireworks brought in the new Millennium. We flew upstairs to view the display from our bedroom window – I flung it open, craning my neck to watch this spectacular light show! It was nothing like any firework demonstration I had ever seen! All around the house and in every direction of the compass, fireworks were being let off – rockets, bangers and many others of all descriptions. The whole country around blazed with a kaleidoscope of colours! Portsmouth and Southampton fireworks lit up the south western sky – It was awesome. A succession of bangs, like machine gun fire, lasted some twenty to 30 minutes – the noise reached us in a kind of rolling thunder! It was as if a succession of bombs were going off! The whole spectacular scene was strange – almost spooky, in a funny type of way! An experience that I may never witness again.

The – [Rowlands Castle, Hampshire.] Millennium 2000 – photo shoot organised for 12.45pm, on the village green. At 12.15 the villagers filed out of church and onto the village green, where there, was planted the Christmas tree. Here they all took part in an open air church service! While this service was in progress, I made myself busy, deciding on the best place to take their photograph. Met Francesca Wade-Palmer, who had organised the photo shoot. I estimated there were around 1,500 people present for the photograph. Took some time to get them all organised for the picture! I had to commandeer an old model 'T' Ford that they had on the green, which was part of their Christmas event. Standing the ladder on the back of this old flat-bed lorry, gave me enough height to take the photo! All seemed pleased with the event.

16th January – [Kirdford.] Dull, cloudy weather this morning – cleared up to a lovely bright day this afternoon. At about 11.am we drove over to Kirdford – parked up in the lane that leads down to Wephurst Park Farm. From here we set off on our ramble – saw some fieldfares, a robin, and a wren. Wandered through the damp woods – catkins out already – Sue picked a few twigs. I peered into the old tithe barn that

Mr Knight's father (the gamekeeper) told us about – then we carried on – following the footpath round in a circular walk back to the car. Drove to the entrance of Crouchland Farm, and set off down the lane – but before long, we found it too muddy to go any further – so turned back. A couple of dogs sprang out from the farm at us – angry, viscous looking animals – we diverged onto another path. And from there, we spotted an old, unconverted barn, [Hardnip's Barn] way across the fields: tramped over to it and took a few photos; then made our way back to the car. It was a most relaxing country walk. Pulled into Rumbolds Farm, on our way home, and there Sue brought some fresh milk, cream and chutney.

13ᵗʰ February – [Petworth.] Cloudy this morning – but thankfully, dry. Looks brighter over towards the north-west – so it may come out nice later. Drove to Fox Hill, and parked up in Blackbrook Lane. Took a walk down through Pondtail Copse, to Moor Farm – circled round the woods and lakes, then back to the car. A crisp, still afternoon: most tranquil. We spotted an hot-air balloon sailing way up above us. The air smelt fresh and clean – a hint of silage drifted over from the farmyard, putting us in mind of long gone country days. Back to the car, and made our way over to [Tillington] River. From here, we set off from the top of the hill – walked round and down 'Janes Lane' – many snowdrops fully out, the banks and copses full of them – sheets of white blooms everywhere. On passing by the very old house opposite Little River Farm, in Jane's Lane, I got talking to the owner – John Reid. He said he had researched his house back to the 14ᵗʰ century. The dwelling certainly has some very old, and well worked masonry within it. I told him that I thought perhaps the unusual stones built into his garden wall, may well be from the 'lost' chapel of River. He agreed with me. We wandered on down the lane, then crossed over a stile leading into a lovely old meadow; the view was spectacular – so peaceful, amidst the sounds of early spring birds – far from those madding crowds.

20ᵗʰ February – [Kirdford.] Most beautiful sunny day, following a frosty night. We set off along the winding paths from Kirdford, towards 'Gownfold Farm' – and what a beautiful walk it was – followed the river a little way – picturesque meadows; long narrow fields, fringed with crooked hedges that rise and fall – dip and turn with the contours of the ground. The farm was to my great surprise, still as old fashioned as it had always been. A barn owl, startled at our approach, flew from one of the barns; cows and calves peered out from their pens inquisitively. The old ivy clad farm buildings made a beautiful photo! We tramped on down a winding lane, then branched off into a long narrow meadow, where gently glided a tiny stream. Sue noticed half a dozen deer bolting across a distant field. The day was quiet; with a stillness in the air – wonderfully sunny. We lingered for some long while, by an old five bar gate, taking in the peace of the moment. Across the next field, about halfway out, I idly watched an animal foraging! What was it? I drew Sue's attention to it – the beast caught our scent, turned and slunk off down towards the river. For all the world it looked like an otter – far too large to be any of the weasel species. It was either an otter or a mink: though Sue and I are both sure it was the former. The lanes full of catkins. Drove on over to Glatting Farm, [Sutton, West Sussex.] from where we went for a walk down the lane – a few clumps of primroses in bloom; snowdrops are out – a beautiful bouquet of spring flowers. We wandered on over the fields towards Bignor – walked almost there. Both feeling pretty tired, so plodded back towards the farm – washing our boots as we went, in the quaint, burbling ford that crosses the path. Spotted, in the hedge, a beautiful yellowhammer – singing for all his worth – the brightest yellow bird I had ever seen. We found several interesting flints in the field near Glatting Farm. A most enjoyable day – both tired, but fully relaxed. Home by 5.30pm.

26th February – [Clapham & Patching.] Set off for Patching, to deliver to Lady Best, the Patching and Clapham millennium photo print! I was unsure where the house was, so asked a person in the village. Only a few hundred yards away – Sir Richard Best was working in his garden, I gave him the picture, which he asked me to sign. A true gentleman – he came out to meet Sue. Very pleased with the picture.

5th March – [Treyford.] Nice sunny morning – though not so bright as yesterday. At around midday, we set off for Didling – pulled up by the little shepherds church – a great flock of sheep in the field before us, all heavily in lamb. Had a sandwich in the car, then drove over to East Harting, and parked near St Richards Cottages, (I have often wondered, whether these old dwellings may have been built on the site of an ancient chapel?) We wandered down Eastfield Lane, then turned back across the fields to the farm in the village – then on past Hollist Farm, and over towards Pays Farm. The little river that winds down through the valley, has along its course, the remains of a couple of sluice ducts, built of very old stone and brickwork – their purpose no doubt, was to regulate the water that once fed Harting Mill. We did a circular walk round and back to the car – a most beautiful day – home by 5.0pm.

19th March – [Kirdford.] Lovely sunny day. Drove over to Kirdford – parked up by Gandersgate Farm – then set off on our walk down the road. Soon we turned down the lovely shaded path that leads on through Crawfold Copse – primroses out in the woods, catkins, and pussy-willows adorn the hedgerows; all so wonderfully pretty – a delicate trace of embroidery all along the bridleways. Sue brought a couple of jars of honey in the cottage, at the end of the lane. From here, we went on over to River, [Tillington] and took a walk down Janes Lane. Sauntered on towards River Park Farm – then circled round through the woods – birds sang lovely: the fluting of the blackbird was quiet beautiful. Primroses and celandines – a riot of colour on our walk. Home by 5.30pm.

22nd March – [Appledram.] Went to Dell Quay, where we walked over the fields towards Fishbourne. At Appledram, we turned off across the fields to look in the church. Peaceful walk, birds sing lovely – wild flowers out everywhere. Found quite a few pieces of old clay pipes in the ploughed field beside the churchyard. The old 'tea boat' remnants are rotting away fast.

8th April – [Petworth.] Hard frost last night – most beautiful sunny day. We went on over to Fox Hill, turned off down Blackbrook Lane – and from there, we set off on our walk. Primroses, violets and celandines in great clusters all along the way. Turned off into Pondtail Copse and came out beside the lakes of Moor Farm – walked on round and through the shaded woods. Birds singing – woodpeckers laughing; skylarks overhead. Butterflies out roving, comma, brimstone and small white. Most enjoyable relaxing walk.

9th April – [Harting.] Went over to Quebec, where we set off on our walk. Sun still shining, though a cool breeze. We wandered down towards Upperton House; the banks full of primroses. Saw a peacock butterfly. A very pretty ramble, splendid views over to the north. From Upperton House, we tramped down the old sunken path, where the chalk sides are fifteen feet high, with tree's clinging on by naked roots perched precariously atop – its a wonder they ever stay there. Hearts tongue ferns grow a plenty along the natural chalk walls of this damp lane. How many hundreds of years has it taken I wonder, for the natural elements to wear this pathway down to the gulley it is today? A most peaceful walk, in spite of not being any great distance.

29th April – [Newtimber & Hurstpierpoint.] Set off this morning for Saddlescombe Farm. Took quite a few photo's of the barns and of the old 'donkey wheel'. Got talking to Stan Hollingwell, a retired agricultural worker, who has lived in one of the cottages close by the farm all his life; worked there for best part of it too. He tells me that his uncle used to work the 'donkey wheel' and that it was last used to fetch water up from the deep well for the farmhouse, in 1905. He said that he [Stan Hollingwell] used to work with the heavy horses on the farm and that there were several shepherds, with huge flocks of sheep. He recalled walking, or rather driving a flock of sheep, with Nelson Coppard, to Lewes market, then tramping home again to Saddlescombe.

This afternoon we went to photograph Highfield Farm, near Hurstpierpoint. The farmer, Mr. Waters, is a rather elderly man – one of the old breed. He tells me he is greatly fed-up with the amount of bureaucratic paperwork he has to fill in, in respect of running his farm. He has a wonderful collection of old Sussex books, which he showed me – amongst them were several rare editions. He pointed out that William Wood, author of 'A Sussex Farmer', mentions Highfield Farm in his book – the author having lived about this area in his day. Had a job to get away from the old fellow, he being an incessant talker; but pleasant humoured, and with a splendid nature.

30th April – [Kirdford.] Dull, overcast morning – sun peeped out around midday; though hazy pretty well all day – warm too. Went over to

Kirdford today, and walked down Ganders Lane; hoards of bluebells and primroses along the way. Wandered into the great wood, then returned up the track, where there, midway along, we lingered for some while by a farm gate, looking over the meadows. Beyond the first field, in a small copse, a nightingale sang beautifully – unexpectedly. I caught the first, ascending scale of its voice – thought at first it was the wood warbler, but then it continued its unmistakeable song. We brought some honey at Ganders Gate Cottages, then drove over to Fittleworth. From here we took a walk over the common. We wandered through the woods for a few hundred yards – then came unexpectedly out upon a very old house. It was like no dwelling that I had ever seen before. It was, in appearance, no more than a hovel – a long, squat building, with a single row of windows; oak framed, with wattle and daub infills. A massively tall chimney stuck out from the thatched roof. This thatch was in an appalling state, with great holes torn into it by nesting birds, and the ravaging weather. It looked like it had not seen a repair for many years. The garden lawns were unkempt – like an overgrown meadow. [I later discovered, that this old dwelling belonged to an elderly gentleman, who lived there as a recluse in these woods. This 'hermit' – the late Frank Sageman, was, by all accounts, a retired teacher – lecturer. His house, it is believed, is the oldest building in Fittleworth – It still has, according to local rumour, the old mud floors indoors. He is said to have been a fanatical animal lover: lived the life of a person of many years ago, still using oil lamps, candles and other old fashioned household articles. His decrepit hovel has apparently, never been modernised – and it certainly shows. His love of animals, was so great that when a local resident had a tom cat, which was pestering other village cats, castrated, the hermit took him to court for 'assault' to this feline beast. Sageman, lost the case. Not deterred, the old loner hunted through many ancient books and found a 15th century law, in the cats favour. The eventual outcome of this case, I have not been able to find out.]

1st May – [Lodsworth.] Most beautiful morning, though hazy sun – came out bright by midday.

Went over to Lickfold, where we had a picnic. While eating our lunch, a nightingale sang the whole time in the thickset copse. Quiet enchanting.

After lunch we wandered through the woods, along a mossy ride; bluebells scented the air with their intoxicating fragrance; while willow wrens, tits and finches sang their individual melodies throughout the woodland. We came to an open space, where a fallen tree had been sawn into logs, which made convenient seats for us to rest on, and bask in the warm saturating sun. We lingered here for most of the afternoon: all so quiet – restful; refreshing.

6th May – [Sutton.] Went over to Sutton, and set off on our walk across the fields to Bignor – very muddy in places. We skirted round the mill and into a small copse, wherein I discovered, hidden in thick scrub a 'lost' well, the origins of which, are unknown. The only indication the rambler has of its existence, is by the sound of water burbling out of the fern-laden bank, and spilling into a purpose built, moss covered stone reservoir – which, in turn, overflows and splashes into a babbling brook. And so it was, that as we walked through the quiet woodland glade, I suddenly became aware of this secluded waterfall – which, for me opened out a mystery. Was it, I wondered, built many years ago, as a drinking place for thirsty travellers; or is there a more obscure explanation – perhaps a legend or some strange tradition?

7th May – [Kirdford.] Dull morning, but soon came out to be a most beautiful warm, sunny day. Drove over to Kirdford, called in at Marshall's Farm, where the farmer – Mr. Lywood, let me photograph the old barns about the place. Took both interior and exterior pictures of the farm buildings. While I was busy with my camera, Sue noticed a newt scurrying across the yard – an indication of how healthy the ground is about this working farmyard. From here, we drove to Lurgashall, and parked at Mill Farm. Walked down past the great lake – and over to the barns that lay out in the fields – I was hoping to get some pictures of the inside of this old building but it was full to the brim with great bales of straw. Traipsed back, and along the lane – then down to the river. Heard the cuckoo faintly in the distance. This bird is now quite rare I believe – have not heard it much this year. Sat by the lake for some long time. Very peaceful; but for the occasional interruption of jumbo jets, passing overhead in their climb from Gatwick airport.

13th May – [Wiston.] Went over to 'Great Barn Farm', at Wiston, where we met William Hitchcox, general farm worker – tractor driver of that farm. He allowed me to photograph the inside of the great barn: talked a lot – mostly of how life has changed for the rural worker of today – and the change he has seen in the countryside over the years. "One noticeable difference," he said. "Is the number of wild birds that are disappearing – skylarks and lapwings are not near so common as they once were – and the cuckoo is a rarity nowadays." He went on to tell me too, how much easier farm-work is these days, compared with when he was a young man – and so we chatted for over an hour. We walked on down the lane to Wiston House, then turned off to our right up a lovely shaded, sunken track that led up to 'Lions Bank' at the top of the downs. A most pleasant, walk of soothing quietude. Only the birds as company. We wondered how often Lord Goring, who had planted the trees on top of Chanctonbury Ring, had walked this same ancient path.

14th May – [Treyford.] Very heavy mist this morning – sure sign of a hot day. This afternoon, we drove over to Didling – parked up by the Church: roamed round the churchyard. Many sheep in the fields with their lambs – the little mites skipping and frolicking about in their carefree way. Climbed halfway up the hill and looked back at the awesome views – the great plain of this western quarter of Sussex – captivating. As we made our way back down, a gentle breeze caught our faces; a welcome reviver in the hot sun. The bleating of the sheep and lambs reached our ears in drifting, sweet sounds, as if an echo from a bygone age. Nothing can surpass the sublime beauty, the very peace that we drank in at Didling today.

17th May – [Chidham.] Today, while wandering through the village of Chidham – I felt a sudden whim to pause and look up, to admire the bells that hang exposed to the elements, in the nearby church tower – I noticed that one had a pull rope attached. They appeared impressive looking bells, and as I had never before heard them ring, I stood and wondered at what their chimes must sound like – were they deep bass, tenor or treble? While pondering on this thought, I noticed to my amazement, one of the bells move (the one with the rope attached), it then chimed, and continued to chime for some five minutes. What a strange coincidence. That someone should begin to ring this bell, at the very same time that I was wondering what it sounded like.

29th May – [Steyning] Very bright sunny morning – which lasted all day. Set off for Steyning around 8.30a.m. Turned off at Wiston, then drove down 'Spithandle Lane;' where along here we parked up and walked up this lovely old unaltered track to 'Hawking Sopers:' here I photographed the barn. Very picturesque setting. We wandered back towards 'Guesses Farm', with the clear call of the cuckoo floating across the fields to add to our pleasant jaunt. Took a picture of the Dutch barn at 'Guesses Farm,' then made our way back to the car.

18th June – [Ebernoe.] Warm during the night, woke to a sizzling hot day – bright sun, clear blue sky. Drove over to Crawford Farm, Balls Cross – then we traipsed over to Old Elkham: the sun was stifling as we made our way to the farm barns. Across the fields, at some good distance, we noticed a buzzard soaring high on the warm thermals. Then as we drew near the barn, two beautiful white barn-owls flew out of the building – Inside, there is a 'barn-owl' nest box, so presumably they have eggs in it. I photographed the old crooked beams inside, then we left and wandered back to Crawford Farm, and on to Gandersgate Lane: this old track is most beautiful, flanked by foxgloves and deep shaded woodlands. Across the field, close by, Sue noticed a couple of lapwings (plovers) which I suspect were nesting in the field.

8th July – [Harting.] Had a salad for our evening meal, then decided to drive over to East Harting – Turkey Island, where we parked up and set off on a much needed, relaxing, evening walk. Strolled down the lanes then across the hay meadows towards Pays Farm – the downs looking peaceful, friendly and comforting – the whole scene before me having a familiar, enduring charm. I stood for some while in the middle of this old hayfield, gazing towards the hills. Then we made our way slowly back to the old byway and continued on towards Hollist Farm. Hearts-tongue ferns flanking the road looked pretty. The honeysuckle falling over the wall by Hollist Farm proved irresistible to Sue, she picked a few sprigs and held them to my nose to take in the sweet scented perfume they gave out. The sheep with their lambs appeared contented – much grown since last we saw them: the little sucklings still in playful mood, leaped and bounded; bleating with pleasure at their games. How peaceful the whole scene looked. We lingered on; then with the slow fading light, we watched the lambs begin to search out their mothers – each seeking the comfort and security needed for the long night to come. Owls hooted, and quietness settled for the close of yet another day.

30th July – [Bury.] We went over to Southview Farm, where we met [the late] Ian Hughes – one of the old breed of Sussex farmers; a ruddy faced, good humoured man. He talked much of the old days – how the farm used to be when it was worked by his father. He tells me that the farm was once called: 'Bone Farm' – the barn that stands in the yard, being still known as: Bone Barn. The reason, he explained, was, that in the olden days, the grave robbers, of the district would take the bodies to the farm, where they were dissected – a most extraordinary tale – but by all accounts, true.

12th August – [Bury.] Most beautiful sunny morning. Drove over to Bury, to Southview Farm, where I took several photos of the barn [Bone Barn.] We then walked up through the fields, and on through the woods towards West Burton – we returned along the way we had come. This very ancient path was always known in bygone days, as the: 'funeral path,' on account of it being the route taken by the residents of West Burton, to bring those that had died in that hamlet, for internment in the church at Bury.

28th August – [Crawley Down, West Sussex.] Most beautiful morning – a clear blue sky. Drove over to Crawley Down, where we discovered 'Hophurst Farm': the farmer Mr. Becker, told me he had just sold the farm, for 'conversion:' they are moving out in September. He was very happy for me to photograph anything about the place. I took a number of interior barn photo's; but did not photograph anything outside, as the light had gone – heavy cloud cover – and rain came on. Arranged to go back to the farm at a later date. Mt Becker, tells me that he came to the farm in the 1940's, and is now retiring. The farm has many old agricultural relics – an old haywain stands in the cart-shed. Old seed drills, horse ploughs and many other bygone farming implements are still about the place – a great hoard lie up in the loft above the loose-box, some of which I photographed.

30ᵗʰ August – [Crawley Down, West Sussex.] As the weather forecast for the next week is telling of rough weather to come; along with the fact that Mr. & Mrs Peter Becker, farmer of Hophurst Farm, Crawley Down, is retiring very shortly – I decided to drive over to their farm to photograph it. Set off towards East Grinstead, at around ten to one, this afternoon. Nice sunny day, blue sky, white fluffy clouds. Arrived at Hophurst Farm, around 2.30pm – the sun though, had not yet reached round to the side of the farm buildings that I wanted to photograph. Spoke to Mrs. Becker, who told me Peter was out, but would soon be back. Took a good number of pictures as the light moved round: then Mr. Becker returned on his tractor – I photographed both him and his wife standing by their front gate – a nice picture with the farm in the background. Left about 4.00pm, with a pretty good photographic record of this farm.

3ʳᵈ September – [Amberley.] Most beautiful morning – bright sun, blue sky. We set off for Amberley, at around 9.00am – turned down towards the Castle and parked up in the farm – 'Amberley Castle Farm,' where we met Peter Strudwick. I took several photos of the great barn, both inside and out. This wonderful old farm building is soon to be 'converted' into a private residence.

We then went on over to Lowfold, [Wisborough Green] where we parked up by the old woodland and had a bite to eat. Then we drove on a little further and pulled up at the head of Shipbourne Farm Lane – from where we walked down towards the old farm. The stony track still looks the same as it did over forty years ago, when I knew it as a boy. We wandered on past the farm and down to the river – the old metal wind pump is still there in the field – the river looks much as it always has; quite and gently gliding on its ever winding course. A most peaceful walk.

10ᵗʰ September – [Wisborough Green.] Very misty morning – cleared by midday to a most beautiful hot, sunny day. Around 11am we set off for Wisborough Green – Lowfold – drove to Coldharbour Farm, and photographed the barns, then turned back and parked up by the 'Old Smith's Cottage' from where we walked down the lane towards 'Shipbourne Farm'. Sue was loaded with plastic containers for blackberries – we were busy picking them, when Sue spotted a 'clouded yellow' butterfly – quite rare in this day and age. It was gone too quick for me to photograph, but I did manage to snap a large dragonfly. We ambled on up the byway – photographed the barns at Shipbourne Farm. Then made our way across the meadows – photographed the old 'wind pump' – It stood out like an oasis in the field. From here, we went down to the river and sat there under the shade of a tree – how peaceful. Soon we were aware of the farmer driving his cows down past us, and onto new pastures – it was [the late] Mr. Steve Osmaston – a gentleman, and a farmer. He held his hand up to greet us – we went over to him, and talked of the old days of farming, and the terrible state that farmers are in now. He told me that he had now sold his 'dairy herd' and talked of the time when his father had died – and not left a 'will' and the trouble he had had to go through to keep the farm afterwards, because of the legal system! He was clearly busy, and had to get on – so we said our goodbyes. We dawdled on across the open farmland till we came to an old iron gate – there we noticed about fifteen to twenty crickets that had swarmed onto it. These insects are these days, quite rare. The old meadows about the farm, and down by the river are still as old fashioned as they have always been; it brought back many memories of when I was a boy living at Lowfold. My brothers and I would romp across the fields during long summer days; birds nesting or sometimes swimming in the shallows of the river.

5th **November** – [Fernhurst.] Rained exceedingly hard all day. This afternoon we drove over to see my stepbrother David. It rained in torrents during our journey and continued to do so, throughout the afternoon. We departed from his house at around 5pm, as the weather was getting worse – there being every possibility of getting stuck in floods, if we left it to later. It was strangely unnerving driving up the steep hill near Henley, the trees were overhanging precariously – I feared those towering pines being blown over. Torrents of water were rushing down towards Midhurst. As we reached the 'Old Workhouse,' we came upon several cars ahead, that were having trouble getting through. I slowed down – then drove straight into a flood that came up to the bottom of the car doors – I kept on driving; then made an instant decision to turn off towards Petworth – since I knew only too well, that the water would be even deeper further down the road towards the old mill. We made it home o.k.

10th November – [Compton, West Sussex.] Fine sunny day, all day. Drove over to Watergate House, Marden, where I parked up and wandered up by the house. Still as beautiful as ever up this old lane. Tramped on up to the top of the hill, which has splendid views sweeping down the vale to the Solent and Langstone Harbour. Strolled back to the car and drove towards Stoughton – the byways flooded, so parked up by the river, walked down the way – and took a couple of photos of the flooded road.

12th November – More rain again through the night. Looks like its clearing though. So, around ten this morning, we packed some lunch, and drove to Harting, then over towards Iping – here, we discovered, they had had some bad floods this past week. The water, one of the villagers told us, 'had reached up to the top of the letter box on the bridge'. Further up the road, there had been a landslip, though most of the earth had now been cleared. The river still looks high and dangerous – in spite of it having receded quite considerably.

26th November – [Pyecombe.] Wind blew hard during the long hours of darkness. Lovely bright sunny morning though – wind still gusty – yet not as strong as it was in the night. Went over to Pyecombe, to the old part of the village, and walked up the sunken lane to 'Chantry Barn.' There, we discovered the old flint barn is no more; all that remains is a four foot high fragment, with a few of its air vents still showing. It was disappointing to see this historic old barn had fallen into dereliction. For it is recorded, that in the year 1849 the village suffered an outbreak of cholera – consequently, Chantry Barn, being some distance away from any dwelling houses, was used as an isolation hospital. Eleven people however, succumbed to the disease in that remote building. Sewage contamination in the water supply was thought to have been the cause.

9th December – [Arundel.] Occasional showers throughout the day – strong winds – coldish in the wind. Went over to Arundel this afternoon, where the town had an Xmas fair on in the square. Very entertaining. There were 'carol singers' dressed up in Dickensian style clothes, and stalls selling Christmas fare – such as mulled wine, roasted chestnuts and hot sausages. The most joyful part of the early evening was the 'Mummers' play. They re-enacted this old Christmas caper to perfection. "Here be I, olde Father Christmas." It was good to see such an effort made to preserve our old English customs. Reminded me much of Harry Gilbert, (now sadly passed away,) who I interviewed a few years ago, for the 'Sussex Life' magazine. Harry was the last of the Sussex Mummers – and although in his nineties, he could still recite the complete drama – he knew it off by heart – and just to demonstrate – he did in fact recite the complete performance to me. He almost always played the part of the 'Valiant Soldier'. [I Interviewed Harry Gilbert in the Burrell Arms at Yapton]

14th December – The strong winds have ceased – dry night; dry this morning. The exceedingly mild weather this winter has affected the nature – birds occasionally singing, as if it were early spring. Many flowers, that should not make an appearance till February, or March, are showing signs of coming up. This afternoon, we took a drive over towards Walderton – though we could not reach there, due to high flood water running over the roads to as far as the Funtington turning. Drove back then to Finchean – where the byway to Charlton is flooded – flowing like a powerful river along the whole route for about a mile or two beyond Finchdean – the water streaming right through the village. Much worse than the floods of a few years ago.

23rd December – Another very dull, overcast, dry, cold, dreary day. Quite misty too. Drove down to Dell Quay and had a walk down towards Fishbourne. The old harbour has changed in many little ways. Looks dirty, unkempt: a lot of pollution from the boat yards. That unforgettable whiff of salt air, that was always so identifiable to the area, seems now to have gone completely – replaced by a filthy, oily smell. Noise from the A27 is awful, no more is it the peaceful walk it once was. The old sunken lane – halfway between Dell Quay and Fishbourne, is flooded. (This was once, I believe, part of a Roman road that continued across what is now the tidal estuary.) The first time I have ever seen it so. The River Lavant, flooding the Appledram road, has now subsided sufficiently to allow traffic to drive through. Though still much water over the meadows – which in fact, resemble a lake, more than several fields.

2001

14th January – [Petworth.] Another lovely sunny day, though still a biting wind. Drove to Byworth, parked near the pub and set off on our little walk. Snowdrops on a bank beside a garden wall – out in full bloom. We tramped down past High Hoes, and on as far as Woodruffs Farm, then turned back. A most beautiful red sunset this evening.

18th February – [Harting.] Fine day – hazy sun. This afternoon, we drove to Harting – to Quebec, where we parked up and set off on our walk. We wandered up past Hill Ash Farm, and on to Upperton – the roadside banks were white with snowdrops – catkins hanging in clusters. It was nice to get out for an airing. We retraced our steps a little way, then turned towards Goose Green. Water still floats about the fields: the birds begin to sing: heard a skylark: many finches and bluetits chirping in the hedgerows. Walked as far as the river, which flows gently down from Hurst Mill, and through Hurst Hanger – we then made our way back to the car. A most relaxing ramble.

24th March – [Sutton, West Sussex.] Cloudy – dreary weather – though mild. Drove over to Sutton, parked up by the church, and set off on our walk. We wandered down the lovely old byway that leads to Glatting farm – hoards of primroses along this sunken lane. All the footpaths are closed, due to the outbreak of 'Foot and Mouth' disease. Water lies heavy in the fields – it runs off in torrents, escaping through the land-drains, and spilling out along the roadside banks like miniature waterfalls.

2nd April – [Billingshurst.] Fine sunny morning, though a little hazy. In spite of the weak sunlight, I decided to drive over to 'Oakhurst Farm', to take a few pictures of the barns. Arrived there about 9.30am and met Mr. & Mrs. Drabble; a most helpful, obliging couple, very interested in the barn book project, and very keen to help, by letting me photograph their barns and the old 'dovecote.' The farmhouse is a lovely old Elizabethan dwelling. After the 'photo shoot' I was asked into the kitchen, and there we sipped tea, and chatted about the 'foot and mouth' problem, and the politics that go with living in the countryside nowadays. We all got on very well. Mrs. Drabble showed me around the inside of the house. The great front door, was quite something – it was made of oak, and as old as the house – mid sixteenth century; with iron studs, original hinges, locks and bolts. There was, built into this ancient doorway, another much smaller entrance, which would have been the one most often used in days gone by. The house was built by the Goring family.

12th May – [Northchapel.] Awake this morning, a little before 4.0.am – I lay there, in bed, listening to the birds bursting into their early songs. The 'dawn chorus' is nothing like it once was – it no longer has that inexplicable 'fervour' – that intensity of sound, which always gave the impression that every individual bird was competing with its neighbour – jostling for the most profound and highest notes. But still, it was nice to hear their early strains.

We set off for Northchapel, this morning, as the weather was so warm, with a beautiful clear blue sky. Parked up close to the village hall, and set off up the lane, passing Garlands, and Peacocks Farm, then on towards Mitchel Park Farm. Such a picturesque byway – very pretty, with all the wild flowers out along the roadside banks. Birds sang lovely; though we could hear no rooks; no cuckoo; and no nightingale in the woods – no skylarks out above the fields either. Where are all our favourite songsters gone? Have modern farming methods dealt them a blow?

We strolled back to the car, and drove to Lickfold, [Lodsworth,] where, in the woods we finally heard the nightingale.

19th May – [Harting.] Dull, overcast day. This afternoon, we drove over to East Harting, and took a walk around the old lanes. Birds sang lovely – heard, for the first time this year, the cuckoo: rooks cawing – church bells chiming – a whole host of country sounds.

3rd June – [Wisborough Green.] Beautiful day. Drove to Wisborough Green – and from there I went to Rowner farm, to ask permission to take a few photographs of the farm buildings. Abandoned that idea, as the place had – bright red, 'Foot and Mouth' notices still up – which even forbid the postman entering. We went on over to Lowfold – no foot and mouth notices there – so we wandered on up the shaded lane and out across the fields to the river. A most beautiful walk – all the meadows a carpet of yellow buttercups – it all looked so very old fashioned.

20th July – [Upper Beeding.] Most beautiful sunny morning – I phoned Robin and Sandra Windus (farmer) of Trueleigh Manor Farm, Edburton, to enquire whether it was convenient to take another photograph of their barns, for the front cover of the 'planned' [West Sussex Barns & Farm Buildings] book. They said it would be O.K. We arrived earlier than expected, so Sandra, invited us in for coffee – we talked about the history of the house and the district – she then showed us around the premises. A most beautiful old place with great oak beams of an enormous size: a real unaltered farmhouse. We then made our way to the garden, where Sandra, asked if I would photograph the house, which of course, I was delighted to do. The sun came out again, but the clarity of light, was not sufficient for any good photos – so we arranged to go back, yet again, when the sun may be, somewhat brighter.

22nd July – [Harting.] This afternoon, we went over to East Harting, and took a walk around the peaceful byways: a most beautiful afternoon. While wandering down the old sunken lane that passes by Hollist Farm, Sue found a fossilised ammonite – it was lodged in a piece of sandstone rock, which had fallen out of the roadside bank.

24th July – [Rye, East Sussex.] Another nice, hot sunny day. We set off early this morning for Rye – traffic, as always, was heavy. Parked up in the railway car-park. But, it being Tuesday, most of the shops were closed – as also was the town museum – a great disappointment, since we had no idea that it was early closing. We did however, discover that the church tower was open for visitors – we climbed to the top – magnificent views looking out to the sea – took quite a number of photos.

We then drove on over to Winchelsea – a wonderful, picturesque place. Here, we looked around the museum, which is situated in the 'Olde Town Hall' – very interesting it was too. That which caught the imagination most, were two pairs of 17th century child's shoes, which had been found in an old house in the locality. They were skilfully made with leather uppers – the sole and heal constructed of wood. It was amazing to me, that they had survived the years. We walked about the town – in the great church – and saw too, Ellen Terry's house – and wondered at the times of long ago, when John Wesley, preached his last sermon beneath the great shaded tree. A most enjoyable afternoon.

28th **July** – [Chalton, Hampshire.] Another very hot, sizzling day – possibly more so than yesterday. This afternoon, we drove over to Idsworth. Parked up by the footpath that leads to the church – another large wedding was going on in this little chapel – it appears to be a popular venue for those seeking an unspoilt country setting for such events. We took the track that cuts up past the remains of the old 'mansion,' [once the seat of Sir Jervoise.] This massive house, was demolished when the railway cut through the Squires grounds. He, Sir Jervoise, had refused, for some good long while, to sell any of his land to the rail-road company, until they made him a worthwhile offer – a huge sum was finally agreed – and with this money, he built the roomy dwelling on the adjoining hill: [Idsworth House.] A medieval (roofless) dovecote still survives; as also do the cellars of the original mansion – they are, in fact, spacious enough to fit several double decker buses inside. The great avenue, can still be seen from the fields beyond the site of the old house. Idsworth, up until the plague, was a fine medieval village. From the top of an upland meadow, we watched the 'wedding guests' file out of the church – and walk the well worn path across the field to their cars.

25th **August** – Thunderstorm came in from the sea early this morning. Did not last long, turned out to be a very, very hot day. Wrote a letter of reply to John Gillett, [Director of Winchester College of Art] in reply to his invitation for me to take part in the 'Forest Photographic Exhibition', which I have accepted. Then, at around 11.30 am we took a drive over the Mardens, had picnic, then went to Lordington [Racton] fête – many people there – very hot – so did not stay long.

27th **August** – Nice sunny morning – up by 7.30am. Hope to find an interesting 'tree' today, for the art exhibition at Winchester College. What I have in mind is, perhaps, an 'oak' of great age, with a massive girth; a noble English tree that has some history attached to it, by way of being used for furniture; farm implements; boats; dwellings; barns or something in that line. Drove to Parham, where, in the park, there are numerous trees, some as old as you can get anywhere in Sussex. Walked up the west drive, and photographed several interesting specimens. This done, we went to Rackham; to the little fête that is held there every year. Quite a good, relaxing day.

1st September – Bright sunny morning, which continued most of the day. Drove to Balls Cross, then circled round to Ebernoe, where we stopped and had a picnic on the 'green'. Then we went on over to Selham,where there was a church fête being held in the grounds of Hurlands Farm, garden. A quaint little village, nice people – lovely fête – they had made a good effort, with books and bric-a-brac etc. The farm has some picturesque old buildings, still in agricultural use, which is heartening to see. We looked around the little church – herringbone construction, with a fine Saxon arch – touches of Norman work are evident also. A fascinating little building; though I could see no signs of the expected medieval 'scratch dials'; nor of any ancient 'graffiti' that as is sometimes seen in these old buildings. We then drove to Didling and sat in the field by the little shepherds church [St. Andrews] – the sun was warm, the air pleasant – the afternoon drifted by in serene peace. Rooks soared and weaved over the meadows, indicating a change in the weather. How sacred and wonderful this part of Sussex is – there is no other place so perfect: it soothes the jaded spirit. It touches the heart; the inner soul. It is for sure – "The Spirit of the Downs," that reigns supreme here. It was a long while before we pulled ourselves away and headed for home.

2nd September – [Easebourne.] Very cloudy, dull morning – rain forecast for later. This afternoon we drove to Midhurst, parked by Benbow Pond. From here we set off across the fields to the 'Queen Elizabeth Oak' tree – so called on account of the visit made by Queen Elizabeth I to Cowdray, in 1591 "She came to visit my Lorde's walks" she was conducted to an oak not far off "where on it her Majesties arms and all the arms of the noblemen and gentlemen of that shire were hanged in escutcheons most beautiful" - which is an indication that this particular oak tree was of some considerable size, in those far off days, and perhaps as much as five hundred years old; making this massive and noble tree probably a thousand years old today and still living – just! Sadly it seems that of some recent years it had suffered a lightning strike – the result being that the tree has now a massive hollow in the trunk. I measured the girth, at 4ft from the ground, it measured 43ft. 3 inches in circumference, which is a pretty impressive size by any standards. I photographed Sue standing in the hollow of this tree. Nearby there is a crease in the ground, where it is said the Queen was entertained by various sporting games. The tree is much the largest, most interesting and picturesque that I have seen. Nearby are two other oak trees, with a girth of much similar size to that of the Royal Oak – these two specimens will certainly have been alive during the visit by the Queen. [This photograph was used for the 'Forest' exhibition, which was held at the Winchester Gallery, on Tuesday 9th July, 2002. It was an exhibition of trees, by 28 contemporary artists.]

23rd September – [Harting.] This afternoon we went over to East Harting and took a walk around the old shaded lanes. The air had a distinct autumnal feel about it – quite lovely. The hedgerows were laden with blackberries – the villagers no longer harvest this fruit to make preserves – the jam, and the apple and blackberry pies that Sue makes, are quite delicious.

23rd December – Another hard frost last night, followed by a bright, chilly, sunny day. At about 4.30pm, we set off for Lavant, then on to Binderton, pulled up outside Ox-barn. This house has for some years been lit up with Christmas fairy lights, all set out in the most fascinating way. The dwelling stands alone in the darkness, and looks quiet unique. With tripod and camera, I took several photos of the place, and while doing so, a stream of cars were constantly pulling in to admire the illuminations – it has certainly proved a fascinating attraction to passing traffic.

29th December – Snowed last night – about half an inch on the ground. Drove over to Barlavington – then Sutton – parked at Glatting farm and had a sandwich in the car, then made our way over to Slindon, and called on Robin Upton – he having promised to give me a copy of an old map of the area. A most interesting man – he has devoted a great amount of his time in the study of the village, and the local area. He has a great amount of local historical information on his computer – showed me some snippets – which included the location of a couple of iron age settlements, that were close to Warren barn. [This old barn is in my book: West Sussex Barns and Farm Buildings.] He tells me he has several thousand flint implements – all found about the fields – including a good number of flint axe heads, some of which are polished. I found him a very interesting man, and generous with his information – wish him luck in his future historical investigations.

2002

16th February – [Treyford.] This evening we went over to Didling and looked in the church. On our way out, we met my old friend Peter Iden [the late Peter Iden, celebrated Chichester artist] he has altered since I last saw him. We chatted a while on the beauty of the downs about us. He had just walked down from the top of Didling Hill, and said how wonderful the light was up there – the air fresh and clear.

17th February – Very dull, dismal weather this morning. Drove over to River, had a bite to eat and flask of tea in the car. We then took a walk down the old lanes, and paths to Roundabout Farm, then on across the common. Lovely old walk along here, very quite: birds begin to sing, primroses showing their blooms, daffs are budding out already, catkins all out. Drove over to Westlands, [Petworth,] wandered down Blackbrook Lane – a few primroses about, though not near so many as there used to be.

2nd March – [Northchapel.] While over at Northchapel today, we noticed the old cart-shed, which stood at the entrance to Peacocks Farm, has now been pulled to the ground; dismantled – the debris completely removed from the site. There now remains no evidence that this old farm building, that was probably built in the early 18th century was ever there. The countryside will be the poorer without this quaint, oak beamed shed. Fortunately, I photographed this construction when it was in fair condition, about a dozen years ago, then I took another, more recent picture of it, when it was a tumbledown ruin.

16th March – [Bepton.] Took a drive over to Bepton – a most beautiful old lane, with captivating scenery each side. Parked up at Church Farm and took a look around the 12th century church – very peaceful, quaint old building perched on a mound. Inside there is a monument telling us that here lived and died the last of the 'Scardevilles' who passed away in the Victorian times. The 'Scardevilles' came from Funtington, near Chichester and lived at Densworth House. The churchyard, while we were there, was in the process of having a clear up. Three or four men had cut down the trees and shrubs and had a good fire going. One of the elder men spoke – a pleasant sort of chap – said he'd just scorched his beard, and wasn't too amused by it. Smiling, he carried on with a twinkle in his eyes, saying that when he puts the bill in to the vicar for the work done – "he'd best say a prayer." Meaning – that there would be an extra cost, for his singed beard. The dry humour of this old countryman made us chuckle.

17th **March** – Cloudy, with occasional periods of hazy sun. Came on to rain hard around 4pm. Drove over to Bepton, where we again, like yesterday parked up at the church. Had a very relaxing walk around the lanes – primroses and violets are all out along the banks. Birds sing lovely: rooks squawking in their colonies. Was a nice ramble today. Home by around 4pm – just as it came on to rain hard.

23rd **March** – Sun struggles this morning, overcast to the west. Drove over to Fernhurst, where there was a farm sale 'auction', [held in the barn at the rear of the Kings Arms Pub] . We brought for £20 – an antique wooden bucket, with metal handle, which we intend to use as a flower pot container. Drove on to Pheasant Court Farm lane, [Northchapel,] parked close to the old mill pond and had a flask of tea and a sandwich in the car. Took a little walk through the woods: carpets of primroses: birds sing lovely. Sue spotted a beautiful barn owl silently flying through the woodland trees, nice to see they're still about.

21st **April** – Lovely sunny day. Loaded our bikes in the car and drove to Northchapel: parked up by the green, and set off on our bike ride – sun was very warm. Birds singing beautifully, as we made our way along the country-lanes. We went up past Mitchell Park farm, and Pipers wood: the woodlands a carpet of blue; the sweet scent of the bluebells drifted out and filled the air. Primroses all along the banks. Cycled on to Ebernoe, where near the cricket pitch we stopped for a sip of tea from our flask, and a few minutes rest. A couple of buzzards circled high above us – sailing on the warm thermals. We peddled on to as far as Colehook; then towards Pheasant Court farm. Down here in the spinney, the nightingale sang. Further on, just beyond the old packhorse bridge, we heard it again – singing in a tangle of briers. This overgrown plot of land is where old Carvers house once stood. Made our way out onto Pheasant Court farm lane, then trekked through wet wood and out to Northchapel. Loaded bikes back on to car, and drove to Didling, where we had a little walk up the lane. Most relaxing lovely day – very much enjoyed our bike ride.

5th May – Fair weather, warmish, but cloudy with rare glimpses of sun. We took a drive over to Itchingfield and looked around the church and the ancient priest house – a wonderful old oak beamed building, tiled with Horsham slate. Inside, a tiny staircase winds up to a little loft room. Here in this house, lived in the Victorian days, three families with their children. Which seems almost impossible in consideration of the tiny size of the place. Drove over to Shipley, where the windmill [once the home of Hilaire Belloc] was open to the public. Very beautiful countryside about here: St Mary's church standing sentinel in the village, with the river winding through quaint, old fashioned meadows. We took the opportunity to climb the church tower, this being open to the public. The views were breathtaking. Walked over to the mill to look around it – all so very interesting.

2nd June – Around 2pm we drove to Plaistow Jubilee Day Fair. Took a few photos of the occasion, then made our way to Fox Hill, Westlands farm lane [Blackbrook] where we had a quiet and slow walk down and into the copse and along the shaded rides. Heard a nightingale in the woods, most beautiful to listen to. We saw a spotted woodpecker too – watched it chipping at a rotten branch of a tree – a very pretty bird.

23rd June – We gave Peter Jerrome, MBE, a lift this morning, to Loxwood – where we met other members of the Petworth History Society – there being today, a river-boat trip along the canal. Most interesting along this old water coarse – picturesque in places – I took a number of photos. Peter came back to Petworth with us – we all enjoyed the little outing.

6th July – Dull, dreary morning – not cold though. This morning, we went over to Boxalls Landrovers, [Binderton, near Lavant] – as I am interested in buying one of their vehicles. Met Geoff Boxall, who is the elder of that family – we chatted for some long while – sharing our interest in country life and bygone days. He tells me that he has several spools of 16mm film, which had been taken while working out in the fields in the

1940s and 1950s – an invaluable record of hay making and many other rural labours. Arranged with him, to go back there again at a later date, to watch these old films – fascinatingly interesting.

27th July – [Firle & Lullington, East Sussex.] Beautiful, bright sunny morning – the forecast is for a scorching hot day. Today we drove over to Firle, East Sussex – arrived about midday and made our way to the 'Forge' where we met the blacksmith – Lorraine Philpot, a most friendly young lady, in her early thirties, who let me photograph her at work inside the 'forge'. Met also, George Hufflett, retired publican of the Ram Inn, Firle, – a friendly chatty old boy. Photographed him sitting on his favourite seat outside his house, and again outside the shop. George says he has a collection of old photographs of the area – which I told him would make a most interesting book. He also has some interesting artefacts that he has kept from the Ram Inn – such as the old wooden till, the old oil lamp that hung in the bar, and several other bits. Photographed the Manor Farm barns and outbuildings; then drove on to Firle Beacon,where I took a few more pictures. We continued on to Alciston – I took a few photos of the great tithe barn, and the medieval dovecote. Also photographed another barn opposite the pub. From here we went on to Lullington, [where once, the famous film star Dirk Bogart lived] to look at the tiny church, its minute size being due to most of the place having been destroyed by Cromwell's troops – all that remains is the chantry.

28th July – [Northchapel.] Very hot, sunny day. We drove over to Pheasant Court Farm, near Northchapel, where we sat for some long while by the Chaffold Copse great pond. Saw a kingfisher; hoards of May flies, and a grebe. A number of sizeable fish rose to the surface in splashes – which set ripples off in slow spreading circles out across the lake.

11th August – Although it was mostly dull, we had occasional glimpses of the sun, mixed with a fine shower. Early this morning, we set off for Pulborough [Brinsbury College] where they were holding the Sussex Game Fair. A long queue of cars waited to get into the event – the car-park laying across a couple of fields – completely sodden with the recent downpours. As a consequence, many vehicles were unable to get a grip in the oily mud – some were even stuck up their chassis; which necessitated the use of the farm tractors to pull them out. We eventually made it, and paid our entry fee. But on going in, we found the fair-ground too, was totally afloat – the whole site, where people had to walk was nothing but a thoroughfare of watery slime. But we all made the best of it – slipping and slopping – and laughing as we went. Even the 'Punch & Judy ' show was in full hearty swing; and many merry tunes rang out from Vic Ellis's (from Brighton,) 'One Man Band' – these colourful sideshows I recorded on film. We wandered around until about 1.30pm; then made our way out, and home.

17th August – [Northchapel.] It has been very hot weather all week, and again today – another scorching day. Drove over to Northchapel where they were holding a 'steam rally'. Some interesting old engines, farm tractors and machinery, as well as ploughing with horses – all taking part in the show – so we spent most of the day there. Met quite a few people, some of whom I knew from past events. Took a number of photos – some of Clive Kennett, from Hampshire, ploughing with his shire horses. Photographed the steam engine owned by Allen Eatwell of Wineham Sussex, I also took some photos of Alfred Witherwick (who was busy roasting a couple of lambs on the spit) He being a retired farmer of Lovehill Farm, Trotton.

18th August – Still very warm – though hazy weather. We drove to Wisborough Green, where there was the 60th Anniversary Commemoration of the Canadians who were billeted in the village before going to war [WW2]. Took several photos. Drove on to Lowfold, where we took a walk across the old fields – sat for some long while in the quite, warm sun. Many dragonflies about. Blue butterflies. The thistledown blew in folds across the meadow; the whole sultry scene reminding me of my peaceful, childhood days. We walked on down to the river, then on around the fields, collecting early blackberries as we went. A most relaxing day. Home by 5pm.

24th August – Nice sunny day. Drove to Kirdford, where I photographed the old stone plaque, that has on it the warning on Drunkenness.

['Degradation of Drunkenness.'
There is no sin which doth more deface
God's image than Drunkenness.
It disguiseth a person and doth even
unman him. Drunkenness makes him have
the throat of a fish, the belly of a swine
and the head of an ass. Drunkenness
is the sham of nature, the extinguisher
of reason, the shipwreck of chastity
and the murderer of conscience.
Drunkenness is hurtful to the body, the
cup kills more than the cannon, it
causes dropsies, catarrhs, apoplexies
it fills the eye with fire, and the legs with
water and turns the body into an hospital.]

This worthy notice is set in the garden wall of Gamel House – situated adjacent to the dwelling that was once the 'Black Bear' public house. Took a walk through churchyard, and on over the fields, where I photographed the picturesque barns.

2003

15th January – [Fittleworth.] This afternoon, we finally got out for an airing, and how pleasant it was. We parked up in Fittleworth and wandered along the lanes towards Fitzleroi Farm – catkins were out, and snowdrops. The sun had that beautiful bright orange tone – low in the sky – an old fashioned, 'late afternoon' look about the countryside. Stood for some while looking down the vale towards the downs – the old farm house and cluster of barns about it looked a picture nestling in the landscape. We walked on round to Amen Corner; a lane as old as could be now a days. The sun was going down fast as we finished our walk – just caught the last moments of the day. Noticed a few gossamers clinging to a hedge – not near so many on such a clear cold day, as there once was at this time of year.

5th April – [Arundel.] Warm, sunny day. This morning we drove to Arundel, where we parked up near the castle gardens, and walked to the Hiorne Tower, which I photographed. Back home for lunch in the garden – basking in the warm sun all afternoon. Blackbird in our garden, very tame – he comes right up to us for breadcrumbs. Several other smaller birds visit us too – robins; bluetits; chaffinches; grey wagtail, (which I have seen for a couple of weeks) and some sparrows and starlings – thank goodness not too many of the latter. Saw this morning a magpie in the garden, lovely looking bird, though not good for the smaller birds. Our plot of ground begins to look quite lovely, with spring flowers all out in bloom – Sue having planted daffodils, primulas, tulips and wall flowers in all the borders. The shrubs and trees have yet to show their splendour. Still waiting for the grass to show in the freshly sown section – sowed it last weekend.

12th April – Fine day, hazy sun, cold breeze. Made our way to Fernhurst, where there was a farmers agricultural auction being held in a field. As arranged, we met our old friend, Fred there – we all wandered around the event. Some interesting stuff for sale; which included a late Victorian, early Edwardian, horse drawn cart – two wheeled, with original fold down canopy. In years gone by it would have been called a 'fly', 'gig' or 'trap'. It needed careful restoration, before it could be used – It sold for £175 – a give-a-way price. There was another horse drawn cart there too, but not nearly so old, or interesting – more of a pony-cart for road racing, as they do nowadays. Also, of much interest, was an original gypsy caravan – in great need of restoration. The price of this wagon rose quickly beyond most peoples means. An old land-rover in good working order, sold for £250.

13th April – Bright sunny morning, though cloud and rain forecast for later today. Drove to Wiggonholt, where we looked around the tiny church – a couple of ancient sundials, scratched on the outside walls. Took a walk along the paths – very pretty country. Drove on to Stopham, where we had a sandwich in the car – saw a little owl – many small birds about. On through Pulborough, to Blackgate Lane, and walked up to Toat Monument, which I photographed. Went on to Northwood farm, where the garden was open to the public. The author Pat Hill, being the owner – we brought a signed copy of one of her books, I gave her a subscribers form for my book 'West Sussex Barns & Farm Buildings'. Garden was very small, although nicely laid out.

23rd April – [Dunsfold, Surrey.] Fine sunny day. Around eleven o'clock, we set off for Dunsfold, to visit our old friend Jean Stevenson, of High Loxley Farm. On the way, we pulled in at Chiddingfold, where after introducing myself, I took several photos of the 'blacksmith', David Wright, in his forge – and his business colleague – David Mitchell the 'farrier'. They were both busy working. Very interesting people – David Wright, speaks his mind in a fair and good humoured way. David Mitchell, polite and quietly spoken. An hour later, after some lunch, we pulled in at High Loxley – Jean, greeted us with a very friendly welcome. Her cousin John was there too – on a visit from the north country. Jean kindly showed us around the house – a great privilege – it was like stepping back in time – every nook and cranny was unaltered. Metal barley-twist hooks, where once hung old oil lamps, stuck out from the ceiling; Doors, that still swung on their original hinges, were fastened by wooden latches and ornately shaped iron bolts. Great beams, with strange carvings spanned the rooms. The beamed stairwell rose up to the bedrooms, then on up further to the attic room, where magnificent views can be seen over the surrounding countryside. The whole house was a wonder to wander round. And for me, it had a greater interest, in that my mother's great grandfather had the place in the mid-Victorian times. After our walk about the house, we made our way outside – where we looked around the old farm buildings – two shepherds huts were also interesting – one of which was Victorian. A most interesting day.

28th April – [Petworth.] This afternoon we drove to Coultershaw bridge and took a walk down the old lane past Kilsham Farm. Wandered up past Rotherbridge Farm, then on to Perryfields – lovely old lane – took several photos. On our way to Coultershaw, we met Mr. Ansty, [farmer] who was getting his cows in for milking – he was happy for me to photograph him. He is a man in his sixties – a real character, whose weather-beaten face has a deep copper hue – the wear of sixty summers spent working in the fields. He tells me, he came to Kilsham Farm, 30 years ago. Nice to see the old farm still working

9th May – [Harting.] We set off for Harting – parked up by lane that leads to Down Park – walked on up towards the farm, then over to 'Parlour Pond,' the site of the ancient mansion house, that belonged to the 'Windsors,' back in the 15th century. Difficult to distinguish much of the moat or anything now – all very overgrown. The old Down Park farm had an eerie silence about it. The barns, and animal sheds were decaying from lack of use – vegetation was overtaking the buildings: redundant farm machinery; tractors, old cars and lorries of the 1920 to 30 period looked like they had just come to a halt where they now stand, and there lay rusting. A most strange, uncomfortable place to linger near. We carried on over to Hill Ash Farm, where the wall of a farm building has stone built into it, which is so well formed, as to give the impression that it may have come up from the ruins of the ancient Down Park mansion house.

23rd May – [Lurgashall.] Another lovely sunny day. Late this morning, we drove to Lurgashall and took a walk down by Mill Farm, and along by the river. Quite beautiful – many damsel flies about. Heard the nightingale. Saw the Burnet moth and several peacock butterflies. There seems to be more butterflies about this year.

26th May – Glorious sunny day. We drove over to Steyning; the village 'May Fair' being held today. As always the place was packed with people enjoying the festival. Many craft stalls there; also farm animals and produce. Met Graham Kittle, in the market, he was part of the NFU group, who had a stall there. Said he much enjoyed my book – ['West Sussex Barns and Farm Buildiongs.'] He introduced me to another farmer who lives in Coolham – Tony Robinson (no relation to Tony Robinson, the TV star.) We spoke for some long time – chatting about the state of farming today. We came away from the fair at about 2.30pm, and drove to the manor-house of Wappingthorn. Asked at the great house, for permission to photograph the 'Helter Skelter Folly,' that is situated close by. They said it did not belong to them – so we drove to Wappingthorn Farm – and there got permission to photograph the building. Drove on to Wiston Great Barn Farm, and pulled in at the cottage where old William Hitchcox (farm worker) lives. He was pleased to see us both again – we talked for some long while; he asking me to sign the Barn Book, he had brought. We took a walk down the old farm lane, where I took a few more photos of the great barn. The place was once a most beautiful farm, now sadly, its looking run down and uncared for.

31st May – [Tillington.] This morning, Fred came over to our place, and we all set off for Upperton, Pitshill, [The public footpath, during this period in time, passed through the grounds of Pitshill House: which was, and had been empty for some years.] where we planned to climb the 'Belvedere Tower'. Beer bottles littered the base of the old 'folly' – we climbed to the second floor: but found, much to our disappointment – no steps leading to the very top – they had long since, been removed. The floorboards and joists were dangerously rotten, so we did not attempt to go further. I took a few photos of the place. The great garden at Pitshill, must have been quite splendid in its day: at the far end of the plot, up near the Belvedere Tower, are a group of monkey puzzle trees. There is too, a wonderful little 'Shell House;' a unique grotto, with a domed roof that has a coloured skylight, and two or three windows in stained glass fitted into the circular walls of the building. The inside is however, of greater interest – for tis like a 'time warp' – many thousands of exotic shells, including corals line the room – quite beautiful. On the floor lay two rotting boxes, full of shells – left there for who knows how long – since the last one was placed in the plaster – I wonder? This grotto was, by all accounts, built by the Mitford sisters, in 1811. It was fascinating to see the delicate patterns, styled like a paisley shawl, and pasted around the room. I took many photographs of this unique little building.

8th June – [Madehurst.] Plan to go to Dale Park House, Madehurst, this afternoon – the garden being open to the public. The owner, Mr. Robert Green, sent the publisher David Burnett, a nice letter in response to my 'Barn book' – he has ordered three more copies. Hope to have the opportunity to talk to him today. This afternoon we went over to Dale Park, where I met Robert Green, We wandered around the gardens chatting about the history of the house, and the artefacts that he had found in the grounds. He has uncovered an old cobbled path, and dug up besides, an old axe – probably, by its shape and style – early 17th century. A footrest, that was attached to a wagon or carriage, has also come to light. Perched on a ledge of the hill above the house are several cannons – with a plaque placed beside them with the following words:-

"In memoriam – These guns were the forecastle armament of the Dutch frigate 'Alliance' of 36 guns captured on the coast of Norway in 1795, after a close action with 'H.M.S. Stag' of 32 guns.

Commanded by Captain Yorke of Sydney Lodge.

The father of the 4th Earl of Hardwicke, who on this spot in 1829 parted from his loved parents for the last time, and sailed in Command of 'H.M.S. Alligator' for the Mediterranean. He places this stone to his fathers memory Sept. 4th 1871."

These cannons, we noticed, bore dates of 1786 – 1788. The ledge on which they are placed, Robert Green tells me, was, once a bowling green. The prospects from the gardens are quiet beautiful – breathtaking views for miles around.

17th June – [Harting.] Rained hard about 5 o'clock this morning, but soon cleared over – sun struggles; still warm. This afternoon we drove over to East Harting, and there walked around the lanes. The sweet scent of flowers and shrubs quite intoxicating – especially that of the 'mock orange' growing in the hedge, by an old cottage. Ferns that have sprung up on the high chalk banks look lovely – a profuse growth of hearts-tongue fern. Back to the car, which was parked by the pond – saw there a giant dragonfly – ducks with their chicks looked pretty. This evening we took a pleasant stroll around the 'Shimmings', saw a couple of foxes – down by the river we saw a heron land – he spotted us and was soon gone. Back home by 9.40pm.

26th **June** – [Penshurst, Kent.] Drove over to Penshurst, in Kent today. But a couple of miles before we reached that town, I noticed an interesting farmstead. [Home Farm, South Park, Penshurst] We pulled up outside – and there, by the entrance, we noticed a table with various garden plants on it for sale. An ideal opportunity to stop and buy some, and get talking about the farm and buildings to boot. We chose a couple of marigold plants, then knocked the farmhouse door – it was opened by the farmer, John Frederick. A friendly fellow – full of affection for his old farm – he has lived there since 1938. Told me that 'most regrettably, the buildings and barns are soon to be 'converted.' Though he wished sincerely he had the money to not do so: would prefer to preserve them in their present condition. He was most pleased for me to photograph these picturesque buildings.

27th **July** – [Elsted.] Dull, overcast morning – looks forbidding of rain. Kite Festival on in Petworth Park today. About 11. o'clock we went to the kite festival, sun was out – nice and breezy for the days event. Many people flying their smaller kites – the main ones were: an enormous kite in the shape of 'Pooh Bear' with his honey pot; and another was an octopus. We wandered around for a while; had tea and cake at the food stall; took a number of photos of the event, then came away about 2pm. Made our way to Elsted – drove up to the top of the hill, and then strolled along the track towards Hooksway. Its a few years since we last walked this path – so, on reaching Buriton Farm, we were much surprised by the sight that met us. The lovely old, remote, rambling farmhouse was now no more than a shell – the place was roofless, with only the four walls standing. It appears as if it has been gutted by fire. I took a number of photos of it. [My reliable friend, Steve Eykyn, of Stedham – tells me that

Mrs Woods, whose house it was, sadly died in that fire. The dwelling has since been replaced with a more modern construction.]

14th September – [Heyshott.] Beautiful sunny day – so we went over to Heyshott – to the Country Fair – 'Farming the old fashioned way'. The event, from a distance, looked for all the world, so very old fashioned; with ancient traction engines dotted here and there – their tall chimneys billowing black plumes of smoke which filled the air with the raw smell of oil, and coal. There was too, an old thrashing machine, which droned away most of the day; and a couple of binders, some hay-rakes; cultivators; harrows – and seemingly – just about every old fashioned farming implement that ever existed. It was very pleasant to walk over the fields watching them all at work. Met Dave Hill again – took picture of him. Also Fred Heath from Horndean, ploughing with a crawler Ransome tractor. Ernest Hills from Heyshott, was driving, or rather ploughing with his Fordson Major – a jolly person to talk to – full of happy memories of the 'old days of farming' – he being over 70 years old. Took several pictures of the 'Bicknells' steam engines, driving the belt for the circular saw they were using.

18th October – Hazy weather today. This afternoon, around 3.30pm we walked to the Rectory, to meet the vicar of Petworth Church [the late David Pollard] who has kindly allowed me to take a few photos of the old town, from the top of the church tower. The sun was just about right. The climb in places was a little precarious. Took quite a number of photos – looking towards all corners of the compass. Spectacular views all around.

15th November – The early morning mist that lays along the river, which runs from Midhurst through to Duncton and beyond looks at times, quite beautiful in the morning. On one particular day, it lay in fluffy coils that curled all along the stretch of the river – and from a distance, with the sun highlighting the hills that protruded above – it appeared quite enchanting. Sometimes it stretches along the same route – like a ribbon, hovering above the ground some fifteen or so feet in wisps, as if it were delicate strands of cotton waving gently – appearing almost transparent.

28th December – Drove to Pheasant Court Farm, where we parked up and walked to the site of the old Colehook Mill – took a number of photos. The great pond and mill race, are now, after the recent heavy rains, very dangerous – water gushed in torrents from the outflow. We walked around the woodland paths, saw a tawny owl – large silent bird – wandered back to the car and then drove on home for lunch.

The Diaries come to an end here – other projects demanding my time – not least, the writing of my books :– 'City Streets to Sussex Lanes:' and 'The Restless Miller.'

However – it is my hope, that the above nature notes will inspire others to go out and wander the wonderful field paths of Sussex – soak up the beauty of that countryside – and too, take a few photographs besides.

The sun cuts shafts of light through an early morning mist on a bridle path close to Locks Ash.